ERNEST HEMINGWAY

THE OLD MAN AND THE SEA

with Essays in Criticism

Annotated with Critical Introduction
by Kim, Byung-chul

Shinasa

The successful author

Biographical episodes on the screen:
Hemingway's experiences at the front in the first film version of the novel *A Farewell to Arms*

Love in the shadow of war:
film versions of two Hemingway novels
(left, *The Sun also Rises*, right, *A Farewell to Arms*)

E. Hemingway and his fourth wife Mary Walsh lolling in his boat Pilar, which was their happiest home away from home.

E. Hemingway and one of the near–thousand–pound marlin.

CONTENTS

CRITICAL INTRODUCTION

Ernest Miller Hemingwag(1989—1961)는 그가 24세 때 최초로 処女出版한 *Three Stories and Ten Poems*로부터 그의 나이 53세가 되던 1952년에 발표한 最終作 *The Old Man and the Sea* 까지의 근 30년 동안 6편의 장편〔*The Torrents of Spring*(1926) 까지 넣으면 7편〕과 3편의 단편집, 넌픽션 2권, 희곡 1편 등 book-from으로 된 것을 모두 합치면 17권이나 된다. 그후에도 *The Dangerous Summer*(1960), *A Moveable Feast*(1964), *Islands in the Stream*(1970)등을 발표했다. 동시대의 Faulkner에 비교해 볼 때 그 장편의 수는 3분의 1밖에 안 된다.

Major American Writers (ed. by H. M. Jones & E. E. Leisy, 1949)의 시대구분에 의하면,

(1) 제1기는 고교시대(청소년시대 :1889~1917)로, Oak Park High School의 학교 주간지 *The Trapeze*, 文芸季刊誌 *The Tabula* 등에 단편을 기고하던 초기의 습작시기를 말하며, 1917년은 그의 나이 18세 때로 이 해에 그는 고등학교를 졸업하고 있다.

(2) 제2기는 소위 Lost Generation 시대, 연대로 봐서 1917~1936년 사이로, 그가 본격적으로 습작에 전념하던 파리시기를 起点으로 해서 1935년의 *Green Hills of Africa*을 終点으로 하고 있다. 이 시기의 主題的 特徵은 소위 虛無에 시달리던 摸索과 彷徨의 시대로서, 그의 否定的 비젼으로 일관되어 있던 시대였다.

(3) 제3기는 1937년의 *To Have and Have Not*을 기점으로 하여 1940년의 *For Whom the Bell Tolls*를 종점으로 하는, 소위 그의 사상적 전환이 이루어진 시기, 즉 사회문제에 관심을 두게 된 시기를 말한다.

(4) 제4 기는 戰后로부터 1952년 *The Old Man and the Sea* 를 발표한 때까지로, 이 시기의 특징은 否定에서 肯定으로라는 그의 개인주의적 도덕의 극한점에 도달한, 말하자면 이 작가의 성숙기를 말한다.

소년 시대 (1899~1917)	모색과 방황의 시대 (1917~1936)	전 환 기 (1936~1945)	성 숙 기 (1945~1961)
• Oak Park High School 의 주간지 *The Trapeze* 편집, 기고. • 문예계간지 *The Tabula* 에 단편기고	• *Three Stories and Ten Poems, 1923* • *In Our Time (Paris* 版) *1924* • *In Our Time* (美國版) *1925* • *The Torrents of Spring, 1926* • *The Sun Also Rises, 1926* • *Men Without Women, 1927* • *A Farewell to Arms, 1929* • *Death in the Afternoon, 1932* • *Winner Take Nothing, 1933* • *Green Hills of Africa, 1935*	• *To Have and Have Not, 1937* • *The Spanish Earth, 1938* • *The Fifth Column*(희곡) *and the First Forty-Nine Stories, 1938* • *For Whom the Bell Tolls, 1940*	• *Across the River and into the Trees, 1950* • *The Old Man and the Sea, 1952* • *The Dangerous Summer, 1960* • *A Moveable Feast, 1964* • *Islands in the Stream, 1970*

시대구분을 중심으로 한 Hemingway의 저작일람은 위에서 본 바와 같다.

1. 제1기—고교시대(1899~1917)

이 제1기는 Oak Park High School을 졸업한 후 그해 가을에 Kansas City에 사는 숙부 Tyler Hemingway의 추천에 의하여 同市의 신문 *Star*紙의 기자가 되기까지, 그의 소년시대의 습작기를 말한다.

Hemingway는 1899년 7월 21일 Illinois州 Chicago 郊外의 Oak Park에서 태어났다. 이 Oak Park라는 마을에는 술집이라고는 하나도 없고, 고작 있다는 것이 학교와 교회 뿐으로 그 분위기가 지극히 청교도적인 마을이었다. 그래서 마을 사람들은 자기네의 마을을 〈世界 中流의 首都〉라고 부르고 있었다.

Hemingway의 家系를 따져 보면 1634년에 영국으로부터 건너와서 Massachusetts州 Duxburg에 정착한 Ralph Hemingway를 미국 최초의 조상으로 하여 Ralph-Jacob-Allen-Anson-Clorence-Ernest에 이른다. Hemingway의 부친 Clarence Edmonds Hemingway는 Chicago의 Rush Medical College(Chicago의과대학의 前身)을 나온 산부인과 의사로, 그는 일생 동안에 약 3천명 가량의 애를 받았다고 한다. 이 부친은 체격이 건장하고 턱수염을 기른 인물로, 사냥과 낚시질에 비상한 정열을 기울이고 있었다.

모친인 Grace Hall Hemingway는 신앙심이 돈독한 the First Congregational Church의 soloist였으며, 집에다 concert stage가 딸린 30피이트 평방의 음악실을 비치할 정도로 예술적 기질이 뛰어난 여성이었다.

이처럼 부모는 그 성격을 서로 달리하고 있었으며, 아들을 자기

들 방식 대로의 인간으로 만들려고 노력했다. 사실 Hemingway는 내성적인 모친보다는 행동적인 부친을 따랐다. 이 부친과 동일한 행동적인 인물로 변모해 가는 것을 볼 때 이 부자간에 놓인 공감대를 느낄 수 있다.

가정에는 Ernest 외에 네 명의 자매와 한 명의 동생 —Marcelline(姉)—Ernest—Ursula(妹)—Madelaine(妹)—Caroline(妹) — Leicester(弟)—이 있었다.

그러니까 그는 손위로 누이 하나를 두고 태어난 장남이었다. 그리고 여름이 되면 一家는 Michigan州 Walloon Lake湖畔으로 피서를 가곤 했는데 그곳은 낚시질과 사냥에 둘도 없이 좋은 곳이었다. 이 피서지에서 Hemingway는 언제나 유쾌했다. 물론 Hemingway에게는 이 Walloon Lake의 생활 외에도 그것과 병행하여 영위된 Oak Park의 생활이 있었을 것이지만, 이상하게도 전자에 관해서는 Nick Adams의 생활과 체험 속에 표현되고 있으나, 후자에 관해서는 그의 어느 작품에도 나오지 않는다.

그의 高校時節의 활동은 눈부신 바가 있었다. 학교 축구팀의 R. G.를 맡아 보았고, 또 수영부에도 관계했으며, 육상부의 매니저였고, 학교 오케스트라에도 참가했으며, 弁論部員이기도 했고, 사냥 클럽에도 적을 두고 있었다. 이러한 활약상은 미래의 Hemingway를 벌써 나타내고 있어 재미있는 대조를 보여 주지만, 그것 이상으로 우리들의 관심을 끄는 것은 그가 학교내의 저널리즘 내지 문학활동에 흥미를 가지고 그 분야에서도 두드러지게 활약하고 있었다는 사실이다. 학교 성적도 늘 우등이었다. 이 고교시대에 Hemingway는 Miss Fannie Biggs와 Miss Margaret Dixon의 두 여교사 밑에서 습작을 시작한 것인데, 매우 개성적인 글을 썼던 것 같다.

학교에서 발행하는 季刊誌 *The Tabula*와 週刊誌 *The Trapeze*에

기고한 글들을 보면, 후년의 그를 연상케 해주는 文体와 主題가 벌써 엿보인다.

육체와 정신의 양면에 있어 그는 늘 이와 같이 활달하였고, 화려한 존재였으며, 후년의 그를 특징지어주는 피로를 모르는 活力과 熱望이 벌써 이 고교시대에 그 前兆를 보이고 있다. 그는 어쨌든 행복했어야 할 소년이었으나, 그 배후에는 늘 고독의 그림자가 한시도 떠나지를 않았으며, 당시의 급우들은 댄스 파아티에도 가지 않는 이 고독한 소년을 조롱거리로 삼는 수가 종종 있었다고 전해진다. 상식적인 눈으로 볼 때 그 정체를 파악하기 곤란한 점은 그 무렵의 그의 삶에 드리워져 있던 이 고칠 수 없는 고통이다. 동시에 이 고통과 불같은 정열이 서로 교차하는 가운데서도, 그 사이를 貫流하는 文學에의 길로 끊임없이 精進 할 수 있었다는 사실이다. 전자는 약 20년 후에 다른 형태로, 그러나 상대적으로 보면 동일한 고통의 모습을 가지고 그를 엄숙하게 된다. 이 제2의 고통은 "The Snows of Kilimanjaro"를 통하여 그 편린에 우리는 접할 수 있다. 후자는 *The Sun Also Rises*가 나오기까지의 파리시대의 습작기에서 이를 엿볼 수 있다.

고교를 졸업하던 해, 즉 1917년 4월에 미국이 제1차대전에 참전하기로 결정하자 Hemingway는 졸업을 3개월 앞두고 징병에 응하려고 했지만, 그 전 권투시합 중에 입은 눈의 질환 때문에 포기하게 된다. 7월이 되어 고등학교를 졸업한 후 잠시 Wallon Lake지방으로 피서를 떠났다가, 가을이 되자 Kansas City로 가서 숙부 Tyler Hemingway의 추천으로 同市에서 발행되는 신문 *Star* 紙의 기자가 되었다. 여기서 후년의 Hemingway문체의 기초를 닦는 데 많은 도움을 얻었다. 고교시대부터 그 主題는 후년의 Hemingway적 基調를 내포하고 있었지만 문체에 있어서는 아직도 장황하고 情緖에 젖어, 쓸데없는 贅肉을 다분히 가지고 있었다. 이와 같은 Hemingway에게 *Star*紙는 안성마춤의 道場이었다.

왜냐하면 同紙는 기사를 제작하는 몇 개의 규칙을 세워서 견습 기자에게 엄격한 훈련을 과하고 있었기 때문이다. 그 규칙을 몇 가지 소개해 보자.

그 제 1 조에는, "Use short sentences. Use short first paragraphs. Use vigorous English. Be positive, not negative." 라 했고,

제 3 조에는 낡은 사투리를 쓰지 말라. "stunt, cut out, get his goat, come across, sit up and take notice, put one over" 와 같은 말들은 그것이 보편화된 후에는 설 장소를 잃게 되는 법이니, 즐길 수 있는 사투리는 신선해야 한다고 했고,

제20조에는 "splendid, gorgeous, grand, magnificent" 따위의 지나치게 과장적인 形容詞를 사용하지 말라고 했다.

이 Kansas City의 *Star*紙에서 기자로 일하던 시대에, 그는 고교시절의 Miss Margaret Dixon과 Miss Fannie Biggs 두 선생의 지도보다는 좀 더 次元이 높은 지도를 받게 된다.

2. 제 2 기—摸索과 彷徨의 시대 (1917~1936)

전후 7개월의 기자 생활을 끝마친 후, 1917년 4월 30일에 *Star*를 退社, 同僚 Ted Brumback와 함께 이탈리아軍 所属 赤十字要員 모집에 응모하여 프랑스軍 배속의 적십자 야전병원 운전수가 되어 5월 하순에 유럽 전선에 배치되는데, 이것이 그가 유럽의 땅을 밟는 첫걸음이다. 육군중위 대우. 이탈리아 電擊師団의 적십자PX 소속. 7월 8일 밤에 北이탈리아前線으로 전속. Fassalta di Piave 에서 오스트리아군의 반격포탄 낙하로 부상을 입고, Milan 의 미육군병원에 입원. 요양 3개월 후 퇴원. 또 다시 이탈리아 보병대에 배속되어 11월 휴전이 될 때까지 그곳에 체류하게 되는데,

그때의 勳功에 의하여 약 50달러의 年金과 두 종류의 훈장을 받고는 1818년 1월 4일 除隊와 동시에 11일에 뉴욕에 귀환한다.

그 해 Hemingway는 Michigan湖畔의 Petoskey로 가서 가을과 겨울을 낚시질과 독서와 습작으로 보냈다. 이듬해인 1920년 1월에는 Toronto로 가서 *Toronto Star Weekly*의 讀物記事를 맡게 되는데 여기서 그는 저널리즘에 있어서의 제2의 徒弟時代에 들어간 셈이다.

이후 이 신문사와는 유럽으로 간 뒤에도 깊은 관계를 맺게 된다. 그 해 가을 잠깐 Chicago Group이라는 예술가의 무리들과 사귀게 된다. 이 모임에 대한 Hemingway의 태도는 高校時代와 마찬가지로 局外者의 입장이었으며, 예술가 단체가 의례 그렇듯이 그들이 芸術論에 꽃을 피우고 있을 때에도 Hemingway는 그 모임에 가담하지 않고 홀로 습작에만 매진했다. 9월에는 Hadley Richardson과 결혼, *Toronto Star*의 유럽 특파원이 되어 12월 8일 아내를 데리고 유럽으로 건너가, 스페인을 거쳐서 파리로 들어갔다. 이때 그의 주머니에는 Gertrude Stein女史에게 보내는 소개장이 들어 있었는데, 이것은 Sherwood Anderson이 써준 것이다. 이로써 그의 習作期의 후반부를 장식하는 모색·방황의 시대가 전개된 것이다. Hemingway는 Stein女史, 다음에는 Ezra Pound를 만난다. 이로써 이 새로운 두 師匠 밑에서 그의 마지막 파리 습작시대를 시작하게 된다. 그러나 兩人의 Hemingway에 대한 지도는 그 성질을 달리하고 있었고, Hemingway의 단편을 읽은 Pound는 青鉛筆로 대부분의 형용사를 지워버렸으며, Flaubert의 표현법을 배우라고 충고했다. 이와 같이 Pound의 지도는 주로 技巧上의 것이었지만, Stein女史는 Hemingway의 습작을 보고서, “There is a great deal of description in this, and not particularly good description. Begin over again and concentrate.”라고 충고했다.

이처럼 女史의 지도는 주로 원칙적인 문제에 관한 것이었다. 이러한 師匠 밑에서 Hemingway는 Notre Dame des Champs街의 초라한 셋방에서 양파 스우프와 cahor라는 싼 포도주와 물만을 마시며 피눈물나는 精進을 거듭했다.

그의 작품이 맨 처음으로 활자화된 것은 1923년 1월호의 *Poetry*誌에 발표된 "Wanderings"라는 6편의 4行詩였고, 이어서 *Little Review*誌 4월호엔 詩 한 편과 스케치 6편이 게재되었고, 뒤이어 그의 최초의 book-form출판인 *Three Stories and Ten Poems*가 Contact Publishing Company에서 간행되었다. 이때까지 Hemingway는 아직도 詩를 쓰는 등 散文에서의 정착지를 정하지 못한 채, 모색에 종지부를 찍지 못한 흔적이 역력히 보이며, 유럽 각지로의 방황도 여전히 계속된다. 그에게 있어 중요한 文体도 아직은 확립되었다고 할 수 없다. 기자생활을 단념하고 1924년 1월에 파리로 세번째 건너왔을 때에도 유럽 각지에로의 彷徨旅行은 계속되고 있었고, 그와 동시에 창작활동에 대한 줄기찬 모색도 점점 활발해 갔다. 1월에 창간된 *Transatlantic Review*誌의 主筆 F. Madox 아래서 편집부원이 되어 同誌 4월호에 단편을 발표하고 또 같은 무렵 지난해에 이미 완성을 보았던 파리版 *In Our Time*을 출판하였다. 이 18편의 小品이 미국판 *In Our Time*의 前篇이 되어 그 本文과 함께 그의 문체의 極限点을 장식하게 되는 것인데, 그 문체를 완성하기 직전까지의 습작이 바로 이 작품집이라고 할 때, 이 작품집의 출간은 그야말로 파리에서 습작기를 보낸 Hemingway에 있어서는 하나의 기념비라 할 것이다. 1925년에는 미국판 *In Our Time*이 출간되는데, 이 작품은 Hemingway 문학의 성장과정을 볼 때 이때까지의 습작기에 終止符를 찍는 金字塔과 같은 존재였으며, 이로써 그의 문체는 완성되었고, 主題面에서 볼 때에도, 이후에 나오는 그의 장편이 이 단편집 중의 단편과 유사하고 단편이 갖는 주제를 연장한 것에 지나지 않는다는 점에서 또다른 중요성을 갖는다. 바꿔 말하면 이 단편집의 출현을 分水嶺으로 하여 Hemingway의 창작력은 가장 충실하고 의욕적인 창조의 시대로 들어서게 되며, Lost Generation적 主題의 세계는 Hemingway가 이 단편집을 출현시키기까지의 모색과 방황의 끝에 도달한 형식과 내용의 두 세계이다. *The Torrents of Spring*을 거쳐 최초의 성공적인 장편 *The Sun Also Rises*에 이르게 되는 것인데, *In Our Time*이 습작기에 이룩한 그의 総決算이고, *The Torrents of Spring*이 습작기와 訣別을 고한 独立宣言書라면, *The Sun Also Rises*는 이 宣言에 의하여 작가의 内的 意慾을 외부에 비로소 誇示한 작품이라 할 것이다. 그 내용적 특징을 보면 Lost Generation적 主題에 충실했다는 것과, 제2부로 들어가면서 나오는 Burguette지방에로의 낚시여행은 *In Our Time* 중에 수록된 "Big Two-Hearted River"의 연장이라고 보여지며, 기타 不眠, 不毛 등등의 여러 요소는 *In Our Time*의 여러 단편을 한데 합쳤다는 것을 확실히 보여준다. 다시 말하자면 Hemingway는 新作마다 새로운 主題를 발견, 추구했다기 보다, *In Our Time*에 실린 단편의 주제를 再延長했다고 하겠는데, 이 점은 그의 문학 발전을 이해하는 데 중요한 단서가 된다.

이 革新의 書 *The Sun Also Rises*는 1925년 7월 21일에 起稿되어 다음 해 10월 22일에 완성되었다.. 15개월간의 労作이었다. 그러나 Hemingway의 노력은 보상받고도 남음이 있었다. 단편작가로 미미한 존재였던 그를 일약 장편작가로 유명케 했으며, 출판 초년에 2만6천 부나 팔렸다. 비평가 Malcolm Cowley의 말대로 1세기 전 Byron이 얻은 성공과도 같은 것이었다. 1928년 3월 파리에서 제2작 *A Farewell to Arms*가 起稿되어, 1929년 9월27일에 초판으로 3만 1천 부가 출판되었다. 4개월 간에 약 8만 부나 팔린 대성공이었다.

*A Farewell to Arms*에 있어서의 Hemingway의 발전을 보면, 素材上으로는 *In Our Time* 중의 단편 "A Very Short Story"의 연장이며, 사상적으로는 역시 이 단편 머리에 붙은 스케치 풍의 삽화에서 Nick가 등뼈에 부상을 입고 교회 담장에 기대어 옆에 누워 있는 Rinaldi에게 "You and me we've made a separate peace. Not patriots."라고 속삭이는 虛無感에 직결되어 있다.

이 작품은 일반적으로 *The Sun Also Rises*의 배경적 구실을 하고 있다고 생각된다. 즉, Brett Ashley는 여주인공 Catherine Barkley를 과거를 하고 있는 여성이며, Jake Barnes는 주인공 Frederick Henry를 과거로 갖는 사나이다. 그녀들은 둘 다 전쟁 중에 애인을 잃고, 정신적 공백 상태에 빠져 있는 가운데 육군병원에서 사나이들을 알게 된다. 둘 다 特別志願간호원으로 거기에 있었다. 한편 사나이들도 戰傷을 입고 있으며, Jake가 性的 不能者로서 등장하는 대신에 Henry는 무릎에 戰傷을 입었다는 虛構다.

따라서 이 작품에는 물론 파리는 없고 Lost Generation의 무리도 등장하지 않는다. 있는 것은 전쟁과 그 허무감, 그리고 전쟁과 허무감을 뚫고 살아가는 Henry와 Catherine의 연애다.

In Our Time, The Sun Also Rises, A Farewell to Arms 등의 걸작을 산출한 이 意慾的 創作時代의 Hemingway 文学의 제 2기는 모색과 방황 끝에 도달한 自己世界의 확립이며, 또한 이렇게 확립된 世界가 社会的 視野의 排除라는 否定的 비젼의 基台 위에서 일관되어 있다는 것이 이 시기의 특색이며, 이 특색은 1936년의 스페인內乱을 계기로 하여 社会에 대한 意識的 관심의 세계로 転換된다.

3. 제3기—転換期(1936~1945)

A Farewell to Arms 출판 후, *Death in the Afternoon*(1932), *Green Hills of Africa*(1935) 등의 non-fiction을 저술하면서 아프리카 등 각지로 여행을 하고 있던 Hemingway는 1936년에 勃発한 스페인内乱을 계기로 하여 갑자기 그러면서도 활발하게 사회적 관심으로 기울어지게 된다. 7월에 내란이 勃発하자 물심양면으로 政府軍을 돕기 시작한다. 선전 영화 *The Spanish Earth*를 Netherland 출신의 영화감독 Joris Ivens와 카메라맨인 John Ferno와 함께 제작한다. 内乱을 주제로 한 戯曲 *The Fifth Column*을 썼을 뿐 아니라, 1937년 10월에는 *To Have and Have Not*을 발표하고 있다. 그리고 이 전환기의 최대작 *For Whom the Bell Tolls*가 발표된 것은 1940년의 일이다.

보통 Hemingway의 작품을 概括的으로 論謂하는 경우, 이 작자가 年少한 몸으로 참가한 제1차대전에서 重傷을 입었으며, 終戦 후 거기서 조성된 戦后世代의 절망과 虚無를 그대로 *The Sun Also Rises*에 담고서 문학적 출발을 시작했고, 다음 *A Farewell to Arms*에서는 그 절망과 虚無가 유래한 源流를 모색했으며, 30년대에 이르러 점차 고조된 사회적 관심이 그에게 격렬한 동요를 안겨주었고, 이에 따라 과거의 절망과 虚無感을 청산하면서 쓴 *To Have and Have Not*을 통하여 貧富의 대립과 사회와 정치의 문제를 취급하게 되었고, 그것이 *For Whom the Bell Tolls*와 *Across the River and into the Trees*에 확산·전개된다 —라고 하여, 否定에서 肯定으로 변모된 Hemingway 思想의 발전과정을 추구하는 것이 常道로 되어 있다.

물론 이러한 견해는 견해 그 자체에 관한 한 잘못이 있다고는 생각되지 않는다. 또 그가 30년대에 동요를 일으킨 것도 이상의 고찰에서 본 바와 같이 사실이다. 30년대는 1929년에 일어난 The

Great Panics을 계기로 하여 경제불황이 미국 전역을 휩쓴 바로 그 시기이며, 그것은 사회불안과 労資対立의 격화를 초래했고, 따라서 이 시기의 작가나 비평가는 거의 예외없이 사회문제에 관심을 나타낸 것이다. 그러한 시기에, 말하자면 人間 営為의 否定的인 면만을 묘사해 온 Hemingway가 그들의 비난과 공격의 標的이 된 것은 말할 것도 없다. 世評에 민감한 Hemingway가 이러한 비난에 반응을 나타내지 않았을 리가 만무하다. 말하자면 변동하는 사회정세에 順応하여 사회적 관심을 표명한 것이 *To Have and Have Not*과 *For Whom the Bell Tolls*등의 두 작품이다.

*To Have and Have Not*에서 출발한 사회적 관심이 *For Whom the Bell Tolls*와 *Across the River and into the Trees*에서 전개된다는 논의는 견해 그 자체로는 옳은 것이지만, 그러나 작품을 주제로 하여 볼 때 그 사회적 관심이 얼마나 Hemingway의 본질에 어긋나며 그가 다루기 서투른 素材였는가를 작품 그 자체가 証示하고 있다고 하겠다. 즉, 否定에서 肯定으로 전환했다고 보여지는 시기에 쓰여진 *To Have and Have Not*과 *Across the River and into the Trees*의 두 작품은 문학적 안목에서 볼 때 그 이전 및 그 이후에 쓰여진 작품들 보다도 뒤떨어진다는 것이다. 인생의 否定的 비젼에는 그토록 능숙한 문학적 역량을 보일 수 있던 Hemingway가 肯定的 세계를 제시하는 경우에는 관념적인 常套語로 밖에 표현할 수 없었다고 하는 것, 이것은 과연 무엇을 의미하는 것일까? 대답은 지극히 간단하다. Hemingway는 인생의 肯定的 비젼을 끝내 얻을 수 없었다는 한 마디로 족하다. 日本의 Hemingway 研究家 谷口陸男은 작품이 内包하고 있는 그 장황함과 饒舌의 범람이 어디에서 유래하는가를 고찰하여, 이 세 장편이 다 함께 内包하고 있는 그 二重性을 지적하고 있다. 否定에서 肯定으로의 전환이 자기 문학정신의 弱化나 선전소설에 빠지는 것을 방지하기

위하여 도처에다 対立物을 설정하고 있다는 것이다.

*To Have and Have Not*의 주인공 Harry Morgan은 다른 주인공과 마찬가지로 행동적인 인물이며, 그의 행동반경에는 반드시 죽음과 폭력이 군림한다. 이러한 면만을 볼 때에는 그의 본질적인 일면이 보이는 바이지만 그러나 그의 격렬한 행동에는 생활을 얻기 위함이라는 목적성이 부여되고 있으며, 그 죽음과 폭력에는 그의 생활목적과 관련을 맺고 있는 정치와 경제의 문제가 수반된다. 즉, 인물이나 죽음이나 폭력이나 간에 이러한 요소들은 이전에 발표된 Hemingway의 작품과 동일하지만, 設定된 행동의 場은 종래의 그의 소설과 전혀 다른 일면을 갖는다. 그의 이제까지의 작품은 가정이나 정치나 경제와 단절된 장소에서 행위가 전개되는 것이 예사였다. 이런 작품들이 결정적으로 실패한 원인은 거기— 즉 행동의 無目的性에 목적을 부여하고, 죽음과 폭력이라는 否定的 要素를 가정, 정치, 경제 등 肯定的 背景을 수반하는 장소에 유도시켰다는 점에 있다.

*For Whom the Bell Tolls*도 실패작 *To Have and Have Not* 과 기본구조를 같이한다. 후자에 있어 작가의 본질과 그 表出의 断層사이에 협잡물—수법상의 실험과 活劇的 요소와 exoticism— 이 흘러 들어간 것처럼, 전자에 있어서도 각종각양의 협잡물이 介在되었음을 지적할 수 있다. 아직까지의 Hemingway文学을 떠받치고 있는 것은 과묵함이며, 또한 불필요한 것을 되도록 삭제한다는 것이었다. 그러나 이 작품에는 그 얼마나 많은 장황스러움과 饒舌스러움이 범람하고 있는 것인가! 사실 그는 과거의 어느 작품에 있어서도 이 작품만큼 그 문체가 이질적이고 饒舌的이었던 예는 한번도 없었다. 한 마디로 말하자면 그 원인은 자기의 본질에 상반되는 주장을 관철시키려는 작자의 숨겨진 의도 때문이며, 한때는 거의 否定的인 측면에서만 존재를 제시할 수 있었던 주인공을 이

번에는 그와는 반대로 肯定的인 영웅으로서 독자들에게 납득시키기 위한 필요성 때문에 생겨난 불필요한 설명의 과잉인 것이다. 이처럼 이 작품은 이러한 두 개의 対立物 위에서 구성되어 있다고 할 수도 있지만, 이 두 개의 対立物은 그 대립물을 묘사해야 할 필요성, 즉 二重性 때문에 작품의 성격이 불투명해질 위험도 또한 불가피하게 안고 있다.

이렇게 볼 때 소위 이 転換期라고 일컬어지는 Hemingway의 제 3 기는 그의 문학의 성장면에서 볼 때에는 제 2 기만 못하며 오히려 퇴보의 시기라고 보여진다.

4. 제 4 기—成熟期

50년 이후에 나온 작품은 *Across the River and into the Trees*와 *The Old Man and the Sea*두 편이다.

*To Have and Have Not*에서 명확한 모습을드러내고, *For Whom the Bell Tolls*에 이르러 그 발전된 모습을 확인할 수 있는 Hemingway의 사회적 관심이나 否定에서 肯定으로의 전환이 만일 実体를 가진 것이라고 한다면, 그것은 당연히 그 다음에 쓰인 작품에서도 명확한 모습으로 그 발전상을 나타내야만 할 것이다. 그러나 우리는 *Across the River and into the Trees*의 어디서 그것을 발견할 수 있다는 것일까?

이 작품은 무대 설정 자체부터가 벌써 Hemingway 다움을 잃고 있다. 이전의 그의 소설은 늘 현실 위에만 서 있기를 고집하고, 그 현실이라는 것도 위기에 직면하여 어느 정도의 긴장을 필요로 하는 경우에만 선택되어 왔었다. 물론 이 작품에서도 주인공 Col. Cantwell이 심장병의 발작으로 신음하고 있고 죽음의 그림자에 억눌려 있어서, 이런 상황을 두고 위기에 직면한 현실이라고 파악해 버릴 수 있을지 모른다. 그러나 그것은 생명력이 소모될 대로

소모된 노인이 겪는 自然死의 그림자에 지나지 않는 것이 아닐까? 그의 현실은 이미 주어진 역활을 끝마친 한 인생이 美少女 Renata와의 비현실적인 연애에 매달려서 살고 있는 余生에 지나지 않는 것이 아닐까? 또 이 작품에서는 사회적 관심을 제시하는 표현이라곤 아무 것도 없다. 있다면 Col. Cantwell이 전쟁체험을 회고하는 장면을 들 수 있는데, 그것만으로는 사회적 관심에 대한 작가의 의식적 표출이라고 할 수 없을 것이다. 그렇다면 이 작품은 非 Hemingway적 요소인 사회적 관심과 人生肯定을 구현함으로써 既往의 매력을 되찾았다는 것일까? 그러나 이에 대한 답은 否定的이다. 그 이유는 사회적 관심과 人生肯定을 구현하는 것이 곧 既往의 매력을 되찾는 길은 아니기 때문이다. 다시 말하면, 과거의 Hemingway 文学은 죽음에 의하여 삶을 체득하고 또한 죽음의 골짜기에서 삶을 의식하는 데서 매력을 느낄 수 있었던 것인데, 여기서는 죽음의 골짜기에서 삶을 의식한다는 격렬한 요소가 결여되어 있는 것이다. 물론 죽음의 그림자가 작품 곳곳에 드리워 있고, 또 주인공이 과거를 회고하는 행위에서 죽음 앞에 놓인 삶이 의식되는 것이지만, 그러나 노인의 自然死는 결코 삶의 통찰 후에 오는 것이 아니다. 한 마디로 이 작품에는 否定的 思考에서 생기는 격렬한 삶의 모습은 없고, 그것은 다만 Renata와의 정다운 사랑에 싸인 노인의 회상 속에서만 존재할 뿐이다.

이 작품은 형식적으로 *For Whom the Bell Tolls*의 연장이라고도 보여지고 또 그 惰性으로 쓰여졌으며, 내용에서 보면 Lost Generation的 主題의 연장이긴 하지만 그러나 否定의 격렬함을 잃고 있다고 할 수 있겠다. *For Whom the Bell Tolls*의 연장이라는 진술은 묘사의 억제할 줄 모르는 요설과 過多할 정도로 도처에 나타나는 独白과 회상, 결코 적다고 할 수 없는 연애장면 등이 이 작품에서도 빈번하게 발견된다는 의미를 포함한다. 더우기 *For*

*Whom the Bell Tolls*의 饒舌과 独白이 적어도 否定을 肯定으로 전환시키려는 목적과 필연성을 가지고 있는데 반해, 이 작품에는 아무런 목적도 필연성도 없이 그저 饒舌과 환상이 있을 뿐이다.

그러므로 이 작품은 이렇다 할 만한 두드러진 동기도 필연성도 없이 쓰여졌다 하겠는데, 구태어 Hemingway 文学의 성장이라는 年代史的 側面에서 이 작품이 지니는 価値를 찾자면, 작가가 이 작품의 題名 그대로 "江 건너 숲속에서" 휴식하면서 뒤에 나올 작품을 구상하며 쓴 작품이라는 과도적인 의미를 갖는다 하겠다.

이 成長的 意義는 *The Torrents of Spring*이 *The Sun Also Rises*에 대하여 갖는 의의와 조금도 다를 것이 없다. 말하자면 이 成熟期에 쓰여진 작품 *The Old Man and the Sea*가 *The Sun Also Rises*와 동일한 성장적 의의를 갖는 것인데, 그렇다면 이 작품은 *To Have and Have Not* 이전의 작품들 즉, 정치문제에 등을 돌리고 사회적 관심을 거부하며, 오로지 고립된 인간의 모습 속에 포착된 삶의 否定的 비젼을 보여주던 제 2 기의 문학세계로의 回歸를 제시하려는 것일까? 그렇게는 생각되지 않는다. 둘 다 정치와는 격리된 세계에서 사회적 관심을 거부한 채 営爲되는 개인의 삶이 묘사되어 있고, 또 문체만 하더라도 *In Our Time*으로의 回歸를 보여주는 간결한 緊迫性을 회복하고 있다고는 하지만, 이 작품에서는 예의 Lost Generation的 主題는 찾을 길이 없이 肯定的인 요소를 支柱로 한 데서 작품이 구성되어 있다.

肯定的인 요소를 支柱로 한 데서 작품이 구성되어 있다고는 하지만, 이야기 줄거리만을 놓고 볼 때에는 결코 happy-ending의 작품은 아니다. 老漁夫가 死力을 다하여 잡은 大魚, marlin이 항구까지 끌려오는 도중에 상어의 습격을 받고 뼈만 남게 되는 것이므로, 생각하기에 따라서는 이 老漁夫의 기워붙인 帆布가 〈the flag of permanent defeat〉처럼 보이듯 敗北의 이야기라고 생각될 지도 모른다. 그러나 一見 敗北라고 밖에 보이지 않는 老漁夫의 상어와의 싸움이 Hemingway的 도덕에서 볼 때에 결국 승리라는 것은 "The Short Happy Life of Francis Macomber"의 경우와 마찬가지다. 그러나 *The Old Man and the Sea*의 肯定性은 "The Short Happy…"에서와는 달리 작가가 무엇에 대항하여 격렬하게 주장하는 식의 그러한 과격한 적극성이 아니다. 그것은 全篇에 흐르면서 저절로 생기는 느낌이며, 바로 여기에 이 작가의 成熟이라는 문제가 작용한다. 그것은 아마 Hemingway가 아직까지 인간세계에서만 포착하고 있던 것을 자연 내지 우주적 질서 가운데서 포착할 수 있게 되었다는 점에 기인하는 것이리라. 이 작품에 와서야 비로소 Hemingway의 작품에서 생소하게 느껴지던 바다니 별이니 달이니 태양이니 하는 自然物들이 頻出하는 것은 이것을 시사해 주는 것이 아닐까?

Hemingway가 自我에 눈을 뜨면서부터 그를 가장 괴롭혀 온 것은 제 2 기의 그의 문학적 경향에서 본 바와 같이 살고 싶은 인간도 결국에 가서는 죽지 않으면 안 되며, 생물은 자기가 살기 위해서는 다른 생물을 잡아먹지 않으면 안 된다는 사실이었다. 이 사실을 그는 이제 자연의 섭리, 宇宙的 秩序라는 관념 속에서 비로소 体得할 수 있었고, 거기에 이르기까지는 거의 한 평생이 걸렸으며, 그의 문학의 成熱은 그의 사상의 성숙과 보조를 맞추고 있다고 할 수 있다. 동물을 인간과 対等한 위치에서 바라본다는 것은 Hemingway에게 있어서 별로 이상한 일은 아니지만, 이 작품에서는 그 점이 특히 강조되어 있을 뿐아니라, 또한 여기서는 동물뿐만이 아닌 모든 物象이 인간과 대등한 次元에서 다루어져 있는 것이다. 이것은 이 작품에서 불가결의 要件이며, 더우기 모든 物象이 同一次元線上에서 다루어져 있다는 것은 이 작가의 視点이 말하자면 造物主와 같은 위치에 도달했다는 것을 의미한다. 그러면 〈my brother〉인 물고기를 이 노인은 왜 죽여야만 했을까? 그것은 그가 漁夫이며 어부는 물고기를 죽이는 것이 자연의 理法에 맞는다고 생각하기 때문이다. 이러한 노인의 사고방식에서 자연의 営爲는 그 모두가 肯定된다. 노인의 분투를 헛되게 만들어버린 상어까지도 "He lives on the live fish as you do. He is not a scavenger. He is beautiful and noble and knows no fear of anything"이라고 찬미되어 있는 것이 아닌가. 이처럼 말하자면 造物主의 눈으로 바라본 경우와 마찬가지로, 노인의 눈에는 모든 物象이 同一次元線上에서 보이는 것이며, 모든 物象은 그 존재와 営爲가 전적으로 肯定되어지는 것이다. 따라서 노인이 marlin을 상어들에게 빼긴 것이나, 노인이 marlin을 잡은 것은 동일한 倫理를 支柱로 삼고 있는 것이며, 그러므로 이 노인의 敗北에는 비관이 없다. 있는 것은 다만 至誠을 다한 者의 의젓한 자태와 상어를 驅逐해야겠다는 굳은 결의만이 있을 뿐이다. (We must get a good killing lance and always have it on board.)

손바닥에 남아 있는 상처 자국은 그의 苦闘를 말해 주고, 평온히 잠자는 모습은 그가 이 고투를 의젓하게 참아냈을 뿐만 아니라, 이 고투를 이겨낸 승리자라는 것을 느끼게 해준다. 그로서는 成敗가 문제되는 것이 아니다. 결국 인간의 육체는 모두 破滅되어 죽어간다는 사실을 肯定할 수 있는 세계관을 体認했으며, 그 極限点으로서 "A man can be destroyed but not defeated."라는 강인한 人間肯定에 도달한 것이다. Hemingway가 이 작품을 가리켜, "It is as though I had gotten finally what had been working for all my life."라고 한 것을 보면, 그가 일생을 바쳐서 도달한 하나의 極点이 바로 造物主的인 視点과 不敗精神이라는 것을 우리는 어렵지 않게 이해할 수 있다.

그러나 이 도달점은 인간을 고립된 개인으로서 포착한 데서 얻은 지점이다. 정치에는 등을 돌리고, 사회적 관심을 일체 배격한 채, 말하자면 모든 협잡물을 排除한 데서 이 작품의 統一된 세계는 전개된 것이다.

Hemingway를 한 작가의 성장과정이라는 관점에서 볼 때, 이 작품은 그의 말에서도 확인 되듯이 그가 도달한 그의 개인주의적 도덕의 極限点을 장식하는 金字塔이며, 그의 문학의 모든 成熟을 내포하면서 그것들을 극한으로 고양시킨 작품이기도 하다. 그가 세상을 떠난 오늘날(1961년 7월 2일 오전 7시, Idaho州 Ketchum에서 자살), 그의 문학의 총결산은 이 작품에서 밖에 찾을 길이 없지만 (1960년의 *The Dangerous Summer*은 투우순례기고, 1964년의 *A Moveable Feast*는 20년대의 파리 습작시기의 回想記이며, 1970년의 *Islands in the Stream*은 自叙傳的 작품이다.), 여기서는 *In Our Time*에서 확립된 그의 문체가 한층 더 순화되어 간결한 긴박성을 회복하고 있고, 主題의 문제에서 보면 Lost Generation的인 否定은 고립된 인간의 모습만을 남긴 채 肯定으로 변모되어 있으며, 인간을 사회의 일원으로 포착하여 社会的 視野를 가지고 인생을 그리는 데 있어 *For Whom the Bell Tolls* 에서 실패한 그는 이러한 視野를 배격한 데서 소위 自己流의 個人主義的 도덕의 極限点에 도달하게 된 것이다.

The Old Man and the Sea

TO CHARLIE SCRIBNER
AND
TO MAX PERKINS

He was an old man who fished alone in a skiff in the Gulf Stream* and he had gone* eighty-four days now without taking a fish. In the first forty days a boy had been with him. But after forty days without a fish the boy's parents had told him that the old man was now definitely and finally *salao*,* which is the worst form of unlucky, and the boy had gone at their orders in another boat which caught three good fish the first week. It made the boy sad to see the old man come in each day with his skiff empty and he always went down to help him carry either the coiled lines or the gaff and harpoon and the sail that was furled around the mast. The sail was patched with flour sacks and, furled,* it looked like the flag of permanent defeat.

The old man was thin and gaunt with deep wrinkles in the back of his neck. The brown blotches of the benevolent skin cancer* the sun brings from its

---

* **the Gulf Stream** : 멕시코灣流.
* **had gone** : had been fishing.
* ***salao*** : (Sp.) the worst form of unlucky「아주 재수없는 사람」.
* **furled** : When it was furled. (분사구문).
* **benevolent skin cancer** :「良性皮膚癌」.

reflection on the tropic sea were on his cheeks. The blotches ran well down the sides of his face* and his hands had the deep-creased scars from handling heavy fish on the cords.* But none of these scars were fresh. They were as old as erosions in a fishless desert.*

Everything about him was old except his eyes and they were the same color as the sea and were cheerful and undefeated.

"Santiago,"* the boy said to him as they climbed the bank from where the skiff was hauled up. "I could go with you again. We've made some money."

The old man had taught the boy to fish and the boy loved him.

"No," the old man said. "You're with a lucky boat. Stay with them."

---

* **ran well down the sides of his face** : 「노인의 양쪽 뺨 아주 아래까지 뻗어 있었다」.
* **fish on the cords** : fish 다음에 that were를 보충할 것. 「낚시줄에 걸린 물고기」.
* **fishless desert** [dézət] : desert without fish.
* **Santiago** [sæntiéigou] : 노어부의 이름. Spanish for Saint James — the fisherman, apostle and martyr from the Sea of Galilee. 주인공의 이름을 Santiago라고 작가가 설정한 데에는 작품의 발전과 관계가 있다고 Melvin Backman은 주장한다. (Melvin Backman, "The Matador and the Crucified", *Hemingway and His Critics*, ed. Carlos Baker, New York: Hill and Wang, Inc., 1961, p. 256 참조) 좀 더 자세한 解說을 위해서는 拙著 〈헤밍웨이 文学의 研究〉(以下〈研究〉로 略함)pp.228-229을 보라.

  Santiago에게도 실재인물이 있다. 쿠바의 노어부 Manuel Ulibarri Montespan이 바로 그 사람이고, 그의 体験談이 이 작품의 실재사실이 된 것이다. 자세한 解說을 위해선 拙著 〈헤밍웨이 伝記,(以下〈伝記〉로 略함) pp.317-324를 보라.

"But remember how you went eighty-seven days without fish and then we caught big ones every day for three weeks."

"I remember," the old man said. "I know you did not leave me because you doubted."

"It was papa made me leave. I am a boy and I must obey him."

"I know," the old man said. "It is quite normal."

"He hasn't much faith."

"No," the old man said. "But we have. Haven't we?"

"Yes," the boy said. "Can I offer you a beer on the Terrace and then we'll take the stuff home."*

"Why not?" the old man said. "Between fishermen."*

They sat on the Terrace and many of the fishermen made fun of the old man and he was not angry. Others, of the older fishermen, looked at him and were sad. But they did not show it and they spoke politely about the current and the depths they had drifted their lines at and the steady good weather and of what they had seen. The successful fishermen of that day were already in and had butchered their marlin out*and carried them laid full length across two planks, with two

* **stuff** : 「도구」.
* **Between fishermen** : 「어부들 사이니까」.
* **had butchered their marlin out** : 「marlin의 각을 뜨고 내장을 긁어냈다」.

men staggering at the end of each plank, to the fish house where they waited for the ice truck to carry them to the market in Havana.* Those who had caught sharks had taken them to the shark factory on the other side of the cove where they were hoisted on a block and tackle, their livers removed, their fins cut off and their hides skinned out and their flesh cut into strips for salting.*

When the wind was in the east* a smell came across the harbour from the shark factory; but today there was only the faint edge of the odour because the wind had backed into the north and then dropped off and it was pleasant and sunny on the Terrace.

"Santiago," the boy said.

"Yes," the old man said. He was holding his glass and thinking of many years ago.

"Can I go out to get sardines for you for tomorrow?"

"No. Go and play baseball. I can still row and Rogelio will throw the net."

"I would like to go. If I cannot fish with you, I would like to serve in some way."

"You bought me a beer," the old man said. "You are already a man."

"How old was I when you first took me in a boat?"

---

* **Havana** : capital of Cuba.
* **cut into strips for salting** : 「소금에 저리기 위하여 토막을 내다」.
* **When the wind was in the east** : 「동풍이 불었을 때」.

"Five and you nearly were killed when I brought the fish in too green* and he nearly tore the boat to pieces. Can you remember?"

"I can remember the tail slapping and banging and the thwart* breaking and the noise of the clubbing. I can remember you throwing me into the bow where the wet coiled lines* were and feeling the whole boat shiver and the noise of you clubbing him like chopping a tree down and the sweet blood smell all over me."

"Can you really remember that or did I just tell it to you?"

"I remember everything from when we first went together."

The old man looked at him with his sun-burned, confident loving eyes.

"If you were my boy I'd take you out and gamble,"* he said. "But you are your father's and your mother's and you are in a lucky boat."

"May I get the sardines? I know where I can get four baits too."

"I have mine left from today. I put them in salt in the box."

"Let me get four fresh ones."

---

* **brought the fish in too green** : 「아주 싱싱한 고기를 잡아올렸다」. green = fresh.
* **thwart** : a rower's seat extending across a boat.
* **coiled lines** : 「둘둘 사린 낚시줄」.
* **I'd gamble.** : 「모험을 할텐데」.

"One,"* the old man said. His hope and his confidence had never gone. But now they were freshening as when the breeze rises.

"Two," the boy said.

"Two," the old man agreed. "You didn't steal them?"

"I would," the boy said. "But I bought these."

"Thank you," the old man said. He was too simple to wonder when he had attained humility. But he knew he had attained it and he knew it was not disgraceful and it carried no loss of true pride.

"Tomorrow is going to be a good day with this current*," he said.

"Where are you going?" the boy asked.

"Far out to come in when the wind shifts. I want to be out before it is light."

"I'll try to get him to work far out,"* the boy said. "Then if you hook something truly big we can come to your aid."

"He does not like to work too far out."

"No," the boy said. "But I will see something that he cannot see such as a bird working* and get him to come out after dolphin."

* **one** : one bait.
* **with this current** : 「潮流가 이 상태라면」.
* **get him to work far out** : let him work far out. get는 infinitive를 갖는 使役動詞. him은 소년의 고용주. work = fish 「고기잡다」.
* **working** : fishing.

"Are his eyes that bad?"*

"He is almost blind."

"It is strange," the old man said. "He never went turtle-ing.* That is what kills the eyes."

"But you went turtle-ing for years off the Mosquito Coast* and your eyes are good."

"I am a strange old man."

"But are you strong enough now for a truly big fish?"

"I think so. And there are many tricks."

"Let us take the stuff home," the boy said. "So I can get the cast net and go after the sardines."

They picked up the gear* from the boat. The old man carried the mast on his shoulder and the boy carried the wooden box with the coiled, hard-braided brown lines, the gaff and the harpoon with its shaft. The box with the baits was under the stern of the skiff along with the club that was used to subdue the big fish when they were brought alongside. No one would steal from the old man but it was better to take the sail and the heavy lines home as the dew was bad for them and, though he was quite sure no local people would

---

* **Are his eyes that bad?** : 「그 사람 눈이 그렇게 나쁘냐?」. that bad의 that은 副詞로 like that, so much, to such an extent.
* **went turtle-ing** : 「거북사냥을 갔다」.
* **off the Mosquito Coast** : 「모스키토沿岸 앞바다에서」. *cf.* off the coast of Inchon : 「仁川 앞바다에」. Mosquito Coast는 中美 Nicaragua 동북부 연안.
* **the gear** : stuff, 「도구」.

steal from him, the old man thought that a gaff and a harpoon were needless temptations to leave in a boat.

They walked up the road together to the old man's shack and went in through its open door. The old man leaned the mast with its wrapped sail against the wall and the boy put the box and the other gear beside it. The mast was nearly as long as the one room of the shack. The shack was made of the tough budshields* of the royal palm which are called *guano* and in it there was a bed, a table, one chair, and a place on the dirt floor* to cook with charcoal. On the brown walls of the flattened, overlapping leaves of the sturdy fibered *guano* there was a picture in color of the Sacred Heart of Jesus* and another of the Virgin of Cobre.* These were relics of his wife. Once there had been a tinted photograph of his wife on the wall but he had taken it down because it made him too lonely to see it and it was on the shelf in the corner under his clean shirt.

"What do you have to eat?" the boy asked.

"A pot of yellow rice with fish.* Do you want some?"

"No. I will eat at home. Do you want me to make

---

* **bud-shields** :「싹껍질」.
* **dirt floor** :「진흙 땅바닥」. dirt : mud, earth.
* **a picture in colour of the Sacred Heart of Jesus** :「彩色을 한 예수 聖心像」.
* **another of the Virgin of Cobre** :「코브레 祠堂의 또 다른 聖母마리아像」. Cobre는 Cuba 南端의 도시. 拙著 〈伝記〉 p.318에 있는 地図 참조.
* **rice with fish** :「물고기를 넣어서 끓인 쌀죽」.

the fire?"

"No. I will make it later on.* Or I may eat the rice cold."*

"May I take the cast net?"

"Of course."

There was no cast net and the boy remembered when they had sold it. But they went through this fiction every day.* There was no pot of yellow rice and fish* and the boy knew this too.

"Eighty-five is a lucky number,"* the old man said. "How would you like to see me bring one in that dressed out over a thousand pounds?"*

"I'll get the cast net and go for sardines. Will you sit in the sun in the doorway?"

"Yes. I have yesterday's paper and I will read the baseball."*

The boy did not know whether yesterday's paper

---

* **later on** : 「나중에」.
* **rice cold** : 「찬밥」.
* **They went through this fiction everyday.** : 「이 연극을 매일같이 되풀이하는 것이었다」. * **fiction** : imagined story or made-up story.
* **no pot of yellow rice and fish** : no pot of yellow rice with fish.
* **Eighty-five is a lucky number.**: 数 (key number)에다 symbol을 주는 것은 기독교에서 흔히 쓰는 것이며, numerology of Christianity라고 한다. 3, 5, 7, 40과 같은 数는 기독교와 기타 종교에서 key number로 이해되는 것들이며, 이 작품에서 이 숫자들은 신중히 사용되고 있다. 좀 더 세밀한 解說을 위해서, 拙著 〈硏究〉 pp.230–231을 보라.
* **bring one in that dressed out over a thousand pounds** : 「내장과 먹지 못할 부분을 빼버리고도 천 파운드가 넘는 놈을 잡아오다」. one : fish. dress out : 「고기의 내장과 먹지 못할 부분을 빼버리다」, over : 「넘는, 초과하는」.
* **read the baseball** : 「野球記事를 읽다」.

was a fiction too. But the old man brought it out from under the bed.

"Perico gave it to me at the *bodega**," he explained.

"I'll be back* when I have the sardines. I'll keep yours and mine together on ice and we can share them in the morning. When I come back you can tell me about the baseball*."

"The Yankees* cannot lose."

"But I fear the Indians of Cleveland."*

"Have faith in the Yankees my son. Think of the great DiMaggio*."

"I fear both the Tigers of Detroit* and the Indians of Cleveland."

"Be careful or you will fear even the Reds of Cincinnati* and the White Sox of Chicago*."

"You study it and tell me when I come back."

"Do you think we should buy a terminal of the lot-

---

* ***bodega*** [bodéga] : (Sp.) grocery shop.

* **I'll be back.** : I'll come back.

* **The Yankees** : New York市의 유명한 프로야구팀.

* **baseball** : 野球도 이 作品에선 중요한 symbolism을 제공한다. 그 자세한 解說을 위해서는 拙著 〈硏究〉 p.177을 보라.

* **I fear the Indians of Cleveland.** :「인디언즈팀도 만만치 않거든요」. the Indians of Cleveland : Ohio州 Cleveland市의 프로야구팀.

* **DiMaggio** : 이 作品에서 DiMaggio는 극히 중요한 symbolism을 제공한다. DiMaggio는 stoicism의 소유자라는 의미에서 소중하며, giver of strength and vitality의 구실을 한다. 좀 더 자세한 解說을 위해서는 拙著 〈硏究〉 pp.177–179를 보라.

* **the Tigers of Detroit** : Michigan州 Detroit市의 프로야구단.

* **the Reds of Cincinnati** : Ohio州 Cincinnati市의 프로야구단.

* **The White Sox of Chicago** : Chicago市의 프로야구단.

tery with an eighty-five?* Tomorrow is the eighty-fifth day."

"We can do that," the boy said. "But what about the eighty-seven of your great record?"

"It could not happen twice. Do you think you can find an eighty-five?"

"I can order one."

"One sheet. That's two dollars and a half. Who can we borrow that from?"

"That's easy. I can always borrow two dollars and a half."

"I think perhaps I can too. But I try not to borrow. First you borrow. Then you beg."

"Keep warm old man," the boy said. "Remember we are in September."

"The month when the great fish come," the old man said. "Anyone can be a fisherman* in May."

"I go now for the sardines," the boy said.

When the boy came back the old man was asleep in the chair and the sun was down. The boy took the old army blanket off the bed and spread it over the back of the chair and over the old man's shoulders. They were strange shoulders, still powerful although very old, and the neck was still strong too and the creases did not

---

* **buy a terminal of the lottery with an eighty-five** : buy a ticket of the lottery ending with 85
* **Anyone can be a fisherman.** : 「고기가 많아 고기가 아무에게나 잘 잡힌다」는 뜻.

show so much when the old man was asleep and his head fallen forward. His shirt had been patched so many times that it was like the sail and the patches were faded to many different shades by the sun. The old man's head was very old though and with his eyes closed* there was no life in his face. The newspaper lay across his knees and the weight of his arm held it there in the evening breeze. He was barefooted.

The boy left him there and when he came back the old man was still asleep.

"Wake up old man," the boy said and put his hand on one of the old man's knees.

The old man opened his eyes and for a moment he was coming back from a long way away.* Then he smiled.

"What have you got?" he asked.

"Supper," said the boy. "We're going to have supper."

"I'm not very hungry."

"Come on and eat. You can't fish and not eat."*

"I have,"* the old man said getting up and taking the newspaper and folding it. Then he started to fold the blanket.

---

* **with his eyes closed** : 「두 눈을 꼭 감고 있으니까」.
* **For a moment he was coming back from a long way away.** : 「한 순간 그는 먼 길에서(꿈나라에서) 돌아오는 듯한 표정이었다」.
* **You can't fish and not eat.**: You can't fish without eating.
* **I have.** : I have fished.

"Keep the blanket around you," the boy said. "You'll not fish without eating while I'm alive."

"Then live a long time and take care of yourself," the old man said. "What are we eating?"

"Black beans and rice, fried bananas, and some stew."

The boy had brought them in a two-decker metal container from the Terrace. The two sets of knives and forks and spoons were in his pocket with a paper nap kin wrapped around each set.

"Who gave this to you?"

"Martin.* The owner."

"I must thank him."

"I thanked him already," the boy said. "You don't need to thank him."

"I'll give him the belly meat of a big fish," the old man said. "Has he done this for us more than once?"

"I think so."

"I must give him something more than the belly meat then. He is very thoughtful for us."

"He sent two beers."

"I like the beer in cans best."

"I know. But this is in bottles, Hatuey beer, and I take back the bottles."

---

* **Martin** : p. 에나오는 人物 Pedrico와 함께 *A Farewell to Arms*의 bartender에 직결되는 인물이며, 작가가 가장 존경하고 숭배하는 人間像이다. 그 자세한 解說을 위해서는 拙著 〈研究〉 pp.190-191을 보라.

"That's very kind of you," the old man said. "Should we eat?"

"I've been asking you to,"* the boy told him gently. "I have not wished to open the container until you were ready."

"I'm ready now," the old man said. "I only needed time to wash."

Where did you wash?* the boy thought. The village water supply was two streets down the road. I must have water here for him, the boy thought, and soap and a good towel. Why am I so thoughtless? I must get him another shirt and a jacket for the winter and some sort of shoes and another blanket.*

"Your stew is excellent," the old man said.

"Tell me about the baseball," the boy asked him.

"In the American League it is the Yankees as I said," the old man said happily.

"They lost today," the boy told him.

"That means nothing. The great DiMaggio is himself again."*

"They have other men on the team."

---

* **I've been asking you to.** : 끝에 eat를 보충할 것.
* **Where did you wash? ... another blanket.** : 소년은 노인에게 무한한 사랑을 바치는데, 그 사랑이 어떠한 성질의 사랑인가를 설명해준 것이 바로 이 引用文이다. 女性的인 사랑이다. 여주인공은 없으나 소년이 여주인공의 역할을 하며, 그것은 Catherine→Maria→Renata 계열의 사랑이다. 그 자세한 解說을 위해서는 拙著 〈硏究〉 pp.170- 176 을 보라.
* **The great DiMaggio is himself again.** :「위대한 DiMaggio는 또다시 제 면목을 찾을 거다」.

"Naturally. But he makes the difference.* In the other league, between Brooklyn and Philadelphia* I must take Brooklyn. But then I think of Dick Sisler* and those great drives* in the old park.*"

"There was nothing ever like them. He hits the longest ball I have ever seen."

"Do you remember when he used to come to the Terrace? I wanted to take him fishing but I was too timid to ask him. Then I asked you to ask him and you were too timid."

"I know. It was a great mistake. He might have gone with us. Then we would have that for all of our lives."*

"I would like to take the great DiMaggio fishing," the old man said. "They say his father was a fisherman. Maybe he was as poor as we are and would understand."

"The great Sisler's father was never poor and he, the father, was playing in the Big Leagues when he was my age."

---

* **He makes the difference.** :「그는 사람이 다르다」.
* **Brooklyn and Philadelphia** : 둘 다 프로야구단.
* **Dick Sisler** : name of a baseball player.
* **drives** : baseball hits.
* **old park**에서 **park** : baseball park,「野球場」. old :「정든」.
* **Then we would have that for all of our lives.** :「그가 우리와 함께 가주었더라면 일평생 우리는 그 생각을 잊어버리지 않았을 것인데」. for all of our lives : all our lives,「일평생」.

"When I was your age I was before the mast* on a square rigged ship* that ran to Africa and I have seen lions* on the beaches in the evening."

"I know. You told me."

"Should we talk about Africa or about baseball?"

"Baseball I think," the boy said. "Tell me about the great John J. McGraw." He said *Jota* for J.*

"He used to come to the Terrace sometimes too in the older days. But he was rough and harsh-spoken and difficult when he was drinking. His mind was on horses as well as baseball. At least he carried lists of horses at all times in his pocket and frequently spoke the names of horses on the telephone."

"He was a great manager," the boy said. "My father thinks he was the greatest."

"Because he came here the most times," the old man said. "If Durocher had continued to come here each year your father would think him the greatest manager."

"Who is the greatest manager, really, Luque or Mike Gonzalez?"

"I think they are equal."

---

* **was before the mast** : was a common sailor.
* **square-rigged ship** :「橫帆을 단 배」.
* **lions** : (이 작품엔 반드시 複数로 사용). 이 작품에 중요한 symbolism을 제공한다. givers of strength and purity의 symbol의 구실을 한다. 좀 더 자세한 解説을 위해선 拙著 〈研究〉 pp.179–180을 보라.
* ***He said Jota for J.***:「그는 J를 제이라고 발음하지 않고 호타라고 발음했다」.

"And the best fisherman is you."

"No. I know others better."

"*Qué va,*"*the boy said. "There are many good fishermen and some great ones. But there is only you."

"Thank you. You make me happy. I hope no fish will come along so great that he will prove us wrong."*

"There is no such fish if you are still strong as you say."

"I may not be as strong as I think," the old man said. "But I know many tricks and I have resolution."

"You ought to go to bed now so that you will be fresh in the morning. I will take the things back to the Terrace."

"Good night then. I will wake you in the morning."

"You're my alarm clock," the boy said.

"Age is my alarm clock," the old man said. "Why do old men wake so early? Is it to have one longer day?"*

"I don't know," the boy said. "All I know is that young boys sleep late and hard."

"I can remember it," the old man said. "I'll waken you in time."

---

* ***Qué va*** [keva] : (Sp.) What of it? 「그건 어떻게 될까, 그게 무슨 소리야, 천만에 그렇지 않다」.
* **I hope no fish will come along so great that he will prove us wrong.** : 「너무 큰 고기가 나타나서 우리의 얘기가 잘못이었다는 것을 증명해 주지 않았으면 좋겠는데」.
* **Is it to have one longer day?** : 「좀 더 긴 하루해를 가지고 싶어서 그러는 걸까?」.

"I do not like for him* to waken me. It is as though I were inferior."

"I know."

"Sleep well old man."

The boy went out. They had eaten with no light on the table and the old man took off his trousers and went to bed in the dark. He rolled his trousers up to make a pillow, putting the newspaper inside them. He rolled himself in the blanket and slept on the other old newspapers that covered the springs of the bed.

He was asleep in a short time and he dreamed of Africa when he was a boy and the long golden beaches and the white beaches, so white they hurt your eyes, and the high capes and the great brown mountains. He lived along that coast now every night and in his dreams he heard the surf roar and saw the native boats come riding through it. He smelled* the tar and oakum of the deck as he slept and he smelled the smell of Africa that the land breeze brought at morning.

Usually when he smelled the land breeze he woke up and dressed to go and wake the boy. But tonight the smell of the land breeze came very early and he knew it was too early in his dream and went on dreaming* to

* **him** : 「소년의 고용주」.
* **smell** : 이미 *A Farewell to Arms*에서 보아온 대로 smell의 導用은 이 작가의 primitivism의 한 표현인 바 짧은 문장 속에 smell이란 낱말이 다섯번이나 나온다. repetition of key word에 의하여 어떤 image를 선명하게 독자의 뇌리 속에 넣어주려는 것이다.

see the white peaks of the Islands* rising from the sea and then he dreamed of the different harbours and roadsteads of the Canary Islands.

He no longer dreamed of storms, nor of women, nor of great occurrences,* nor of great fish, nor fights, nor contests of strength,* nor of his wife. He only dreamed of places now and of the lions* on the beach. They played like young cats in the dusk and he loved them as he loved the boy. He never dreamed about the boy. He simply woke, looked out the open door at the moon and unrolled his trousers and put them on. He urinated outside the shack and then went up the road to wake the boy. He was shivering with the morning cold. But he knew he would shiver himself warm* and that soon he would be rowing.

The door of the house where the boy lived was unlocked and he opened it and walked in quietly with his bare feet. The boy was asleep on a cot in the first room

---

* **went on dreaming** : 「계속 꿈을 꾸었다」.
* **Islands** : Canary Islands. 아프리카의 北西岸에 멀리 떨어져 있는 스페인領土.
* **great occurrence** : 「큰 사건」.
* **contests of strength** : 「힘내기」.
* **lions** : 작품 속에서 주인공은 잠을 자면 반드시 사자꿈을 꾼다. 자지 않을 때엔 항상 소년과 DiMaggio를 생각하듯이. 소년, lions, DiMaggio는 각기 일정한 내용의 symbol (그것은 勇氣이다)를 제시하면서, 弛緩과 緊張 사이를 波狀的으로 노인의 심중을 왕래한다. (拙著 〈研究〉 p. 179; Carlos Baker. *Hemingway, The Writer as Artist*, p. 309).
* **He would shiver himself warm.** : 「한참 떨고 있으면 몸이 따뜻해지리라」.

and the old man could see him clearly with the light that came in from the dying moon. He took hold of one foot gently and held it until the boy woke and turned and looked at him. The old man nodded and the boy took his trousers from the chair by the bed and, sitting on the bed, pulled them on.

The old man went out the door and the boy came after him. He was sleepy and the old man put his arm across his shoulders and said, "I am sorry."

"*Qué va,*" the boy said. "It is what a man must do."

They walked down the road to the old man's shack and all along the road, in the dark, barefoot men were moving, carrying the masts of their boats.

When they reached the old man's shack the boy took the rolls of line in the basket and the harpoon and gaff and the old man carried the mast with the furled sail on his shoulder.

"Do you want coffee?" the boy asked.

"We'll put the gear in the boat and then get some."

They had coffee from condensed milk cans at an early morning place* that served fishermen.

"How did you sleep old man?" the boy asked. He was waking up now although it was still hard for him to leave his sleep.

* **an early morning place** : 아침 일찍 문을 여는 음식점.

"Very well, Manolin*," the old man said. "I feel confident today."

"So do I," the boy said. "Now I must get your sardines and mine and your fresh baits. He* brings our gear himself. He never wants anyone to carry anything."

"We're different," the old man said. "I let you carry things when you were five years old."

"I know it," the boy said. "I'll be right back.* Have another coffee. We have credit here."*

He walked off, bare-footed on the coral rocks,* to the ice house where the baits were stored.

The old man drank his coffee slowly. It was all he would have all day and he knew that he should take it. For a long time now eating had bored him and he never carried a lunch. He had a bottle of water in the bow of the skiff and that was all he needed for the day.

The boy was back now with the sardines and the two baits wrapped in a newspaper and they went down the trail to the skiff, feeling the pebbled sand under their feet, and lifted the skiff and slid her into the water.

---

* **Manolin** : 소년의 이름. 이 Manolin이 가진 symbol은 '勇気의 源泉的인 공급자로서 lost youth에 대한 憧憬'이다(Baker의 지적). 좀 더 자세한 解說을 위해선 拙著 〈研究〉 p.175를 보라.
* **He** : 소년의 현재의 고용주.
* **I'll be right back.** : I'll come back at once.
* **We have credit here.** : 「여기라면 외상이 통한다」.
* **coral rocks** : 「산호암」.

"Good luck old man."

"Good luck," the old man said. He fitted the rope lashings of the oars* onto the thole pins* and, leaning forward against the thrust of the blades in the water,* he began to row out of the harbour in the dark. There were other boats from the other beaches going out to sea and the old man heard the dip and push of their oars even though he could not see them now* the moon was below the hills.

Sometimes someone would speak in a boat. But most of the boats were silent except for the dip of the oars. They spread apart after they were out of the mouth of the harbour and each one headed for the part of the ocean where he hoped to find fish. The old man knew he was going far out and he left the smell of the land behind and rowed out into the clean early morning smell of the ocean. He saw the phosphorescence of the Gulf weed in the water as he rowed over the part of the ocean that the fishermen called the great well because there was a sudden deep of seven hundred fathoms where all sorts of fish congregated because of the swirl the current made against the steep walls of the

---

* **rope lashings of the oars** : 「노를 잡아맨 밧줄」.
* **thole pins** : 「노받이 말뚝」.
* **leaning forward against the thrust of the blades in the water** : 「놋날을 물에 텀벙 담그면서 몸을 앞으로 구부려」. blades : blades of the oars.
* **now** : now that ; since.

floor of the ocean.* Here there were concentrations of shrimp and bait fish and sometimes schools ot squid* in the deepest holes and these rose close to the surface at night where all the wandering fish fed on them.

In the dark the old man could feel the morning coming and as he rowed he heard the trembling sound as flying fish left the water and the hissing that their stiff set wings made as they soared away in the darkness. He was very fond of flying fish as they were his principal friends on the ocean. He was sorry for the birds, especially the small delicate dark terns that were always flying and looking and almost never finding,* and he thought, the birds have a harder life than we do* except for the robber birds* and the heavy strong ones. Why did they* make birds so delicate and fine as those sea swallows when the ocean can be so cruel? She is kind and very beautiful. But she can be so cruel and it comes so suddenly* and such birds that fly, dipping and hunting, with their small sad voices are made too delicately for the sea.

* **because of the swirl … of the ocean** : 「조류가 해저의 가파른 경사면에 부딪쳐 생긴 소용돌이 때문에」.
* **schools of squid** : 「오징어 떼」.
* **looking and almost never finding** : 「찾으면서도 거의 한번도 찾아내지 못하는」.
* **do** : have.
* **robber birds** : birds that eat other birds.
* **they** : 조물주.
* **It comes so suddenly.** : The ocean becomes cruel suddenly.

He always thought of the sea as *la mar** which is what people call her in Spanish when they love her. Sometimes those who love her say bad things of her* but they are always said as though she were a woman. Some of the younger fishermen, those who used buoys as floats* for their lines and had motorboats, bought when the shark livers had brought much money, spoke of her as *el mar** which is masculine. They spoke of her as a contestant or a place or even an enemy. But the old man always thought of her as feminine and as something that gave or withheld great favours, and if she did wild or wicked things it was because she could not help* them. The moon affects her as it does a woman, he thought.

He was rowing steadily and it was no effort for him since he kept well within his speed* and the surface of the ocean was flat except for the occasional swirls of the current. He was letting the current do a third* of the work and as it started to be light he saw he was already further out than he had hoped to be at this hour.

---

* ***la mar*** [la ma:r] : (Sp.) the sea의 女性名詞.
* **say bad things of her** :「바다를 욕하다」.
* **buoys** [bɔi/bú:i] **as floats** :「浮標로서 낚시 찌」.
* ***el mar*** [el ma:r] : (Sp.) the sea의 男性名詞.
* **help** : avoid
* **He kept well within his speed.** :「무리한 속력을 내지 않았다」.
* **a third** :「3分의 1」.

I worked the deep wells* for a week and did nothing,* he thought. Today I'll work out where the schools of bonito and albacore are and maybe there will be a big one with them.

Before it was really light he had his baits out and was drifting with the current. One bait was down forty fathoms. The second was at seventy-five and the third and fourth were down in the blue water at one hundred and one hundred and twenty-five fathoms. Each bait hung head down with the shank of the hook inside the bait fish, tied and sewed solid* and all the projecting part of the hook, the curve and the point,* was covered with fresh sardines. Each sardine was hooked through both eyes so that they made a half-garland on the projecting steel. There was no part of the hook that a great fish could feel which was not sweet smelling and good tasting.

The boy had given him two fresh small tunas, or albacores, which hung on the two deepest lines like plummets and, on the others, he had a big blue runner* and a yellow jack* that had been used before; but they were in good condition still and had the excellent sar-

---

* **worked the deep wells** : fished in the deep places of the sea.
* **did nothing** : caught nothing.
* **tied and sewed solid** : 「꽉 묶고 꿰매진 채」, hung down의 補語.
* **the curve and the point** : all the projecting part of the hook과 同格.
* **runner** : jurel, 고등어類의 食用魚.
* **jack** : a male salmon.

dines to give them scent and attractiveness. Each line, as thick around as a big pencil, was looped onto a green-sapped stick so that any pull or touch on the bait would make the stick dip and each line had two forty-fathom coils which could be made fast to* the other spare coils so that, if it were necessary, a fish could take out over three hundred fathoms of line.

Now the man watched the dip of the three sticks over the side of the skiff and rowed gently to keep the lines straight up and down and at their proper depths. It was quite light and any moment now the sun would rise.

The sun rose thinly from the sea and the old man could see the other boats, low on the water and well in toward the shore,* spread out across the current. Then the sun was brighter and the glare came on the water and then, as it rose clear, the flat sea sent it back at his eyes so that it hurt sharply and he rowed without looking into it. He looked down into the water and watched the lines that went straight down into the dark of the water. He kept them straighter than anyone did, so that at each level* in the darkness of the stream there would be a bait waiting exactly where he wished it to be* for any fish that swam there. Others let

---

* **be made fast to** :「～에 꽉 묶이다」.
* **well in toward the shore** :「海岸쪽으로 꽤 들어간 곳에서」.
* **at each level** :「各水深에서」.
* **where he wished it to be** :「미끼를 놓아두고 싶은 곳」. it : bait.

them drift with the current and sometimes they were at sixty fathoms when the fishermen thought they were at a hundred.*

But, he thought, I keep them with precision. Only I have no luck any more. But who knows? Maybe today. Every day is a new day. It is better to be lucky. But I would rather be exact. Then when luck comes you are ready.

The sun was two hours higher* now and it did not hurt his eyes so much to look into the east. There were only three boats in sight now and they showed very low and far inshore.

All my life the early sun has hurt my eyes, he thought. Yet they are still good. In the evening I can look straight into it without getting the blackness.* It has more force in the evening too. But in the morning it is painful.

Just then he saw a man-of-war bird* with his long black wings circling in the sky ahead of him. He made a quick drop,* slanting down on his back-swept wings,*

---

* **They were at a hundred.**에서 they : baits. at a hundred : at a hundred fathoms.
* **The sun was two hours higher now.** : 「이미 해가 떠오른 지 두 시간이 지났다」.
* **without getting the blackness** : 「눈이 캄캄해지는 일이 없이」.
* **a man-of-war bird** : a strong winged tropical sea bird, also called "frigate bird". 「軍艦鳥」.
* **made a quick drop** : 「急降下했다」.
* **slanting down on his back-swept wings** : 「뒤로 쭉 뻗은 날개로 비스

and then circled again.

"He's got something," the old man said aloud. "He's not just looking."

He rowed slowly and steadily toward where the bird was circling. He did not hurry and he kept his lines straight up and down. But he crowded the current a little* so that he was still fishing correctly though faster than* he would have fished if he was not trying to use the bird.*

The bird went higher in the air and circled again, his wings motionless.* Then he dove suddenly and the old man saw flying fish spurt out of the water and sail* desperately over the surface.

"Dolphin," the old man said aloud. "Big dolphin."

He shipped his oars* and brought a small line from under the bow. It had a wire leader* and a medium-sized hook and he baited it with one of the sardines. He let it go over the side* and then made it fast to a ring bolt* in the stern. Then he baited another line and

---

듬히 내려가면서」.

* **crowded the current a little** :「물결을 헤치며 좀 빨리 저었다」. crowd는「배가 물결을 헤치고 달린다」는 뜻. 본뜻은 press, push.
* **though faster than** : though he fished faster than.
* **if he was not trying to use the bird** :「새를 이용해서 고기를 잡아볼 작정만 아니라면」.
* **his wings motionless** :「두 날개를 꼼짝도 않은 채」. circled의 補語.
* **sail** :「도망치다」.
* **He shipped his oars.** :「노를 거두어 노받이에 걸었다」.
* **a wire leader** :「낚시 철사끝줄」.
* **Let it go over the side** :「뱃전 너머로 획 던졌다」.

left it coiled*in the shade of the bow. He went back to rowing and to watching the long-winged black bird who was working,* now, low over the water.

As he watched the bird dipped again slanting his wings for the dive and then swinging them wildly and ineffectually as he followed the flying fish. The old man could see the slight bulge in the water that the big dolphin raised as they followed the escaping fish. The dolphin were cutting through the water* below the flight of the fish and would be in the water, driving at speed,* when the fish dropped. It is a big school of dolphin, he thought. They are widespread and the flying fish have little chance. The bird has no chance. The flying fish are too big for him and they go too fast.

He watched the flying fish burst out again and again and the ineffectual movements of the bird. That school has gotten away from me, he thought. They are moving out too fast and too far. But perhaps I will pick up a stray*and perhaps my big fish is around them. My big fish must be somewhere.

The clouds over the land now rose like mountains and the coast was only a long green line with the gray

---

* **a ring bolt** :「고리 걸쇠」.
* **left it coiled** :「그것을 둘둘 말아두었다」. it : another line.
* **working** : looking for.
* **cutting through the water** :「물을 헤치고 돌진하고 있었다」.
* **driving at speed** :「전속력으로 달리면서」. at speed : at full speed.
* **stray** :「떼에서 따로 떨어진 무리들」.

blue hills behind it. The water was a dark blue now, so dark that it was almost purple. As he looked down into it he saw the red sifting of the plankton* in the dark water and the strange light the sun made now. He watched his lines to see them go straight down out of sight into the water and he was happy to see so much plankton because it meant fish.* The strange light the sun made in the water, now that the sun was higher, meant good weather and so did* the shape of the clouds over the land. But the bird was almost out of sight now and nothing showed on the surface of the water but some patches of yellow, sun-bleached Sargasso weed and the purple, formalized, iridescent, gelatinous bladder of a Portuguese man-of-war* floating close beside the boat. It turned on its side* and then righted itself.* It floated cheerfully as a bubble with its long deadly* purple filaments trailing a yard behind it in the water.

"*Agua mala*,*" the man said. "You whore."

From where he swung lightly against his oars* he

---

* **the red sifting of the plankton** :「체로 처낸듯이 빨갛게 떠있는 浮游生物」.
* **meant fish** :「고기가 있다는 것을 나타냈다」.
* **did** : meant.
* **Portugese man-of-war** : any of several large, tube-like, warm-sea animals having a large bladder-like sac, with a sail-like structure on top, which enables them to float on the water.
* **turned on its side** :「옆구리를 뒤채보였다」.
* **righted itself** :「몸을 본래 위치로 돌렸다」.
* **deadly** :「치명적인」.
* ***Agua mala*** [a:gua ma:la] : (Sp.) : bad water.

looked down into the water and saw the tiny fish that were coloured like the trailing filaments and swam between them and under the small shade the bubble made as it drifted. They were immune to its poison. But men were not* and when some of the filaments would catch on a line* and rest there slimy and purple while the old man was working a fish, he would have welts and sores on his arms and hands of the sort* that poison ivy or poison oak can give. But these poisonings from the *agua mala* came quickly and struck like a whiplash.

The iridescent bubbles were beautiful. But they were the falsest thing in the sea and the old man loved to see the big sea turtles eating them. The turtles saw them, approached them from the front, then shut their eyes so they were completely carapaced and ate them filaments and all. The old man loved to see the turtles eat them and he loved to walk on them on the beach after a storm and hear them pop when he stepped on them with the horny soles of his feet.

He loved green turtles and hawk-bills* with their elegance and speed and their great value and he had a

---

* **He swung lightly against his oars.** : 「노로 가볍게 제동을 걸고서 뼁돌았다」.
* **men were not** : men were not immune.
* **catch on a line** : 「줄에 달라 붙다」.
* **of the sort** : 앞줄의 welts and sores 에 붙는 形容詞句.
* **hawks-bills** : small turtles found in tropical seas, having hawklike beaks and horny shells from which tortoise are obtained.

friendly contempt for the huge, stupid loggerheads,* yellow in their armour-plating,* strange in their love-making, and happily eating the Portuguese men-of-war with their eyes shut.

He had no mysticism about turtles although he had gone in turtle boats for many years. He was sorry for them all, even the great trunk backs* that were as long as the skiff and weighed a ton. Most people are heartless about turtles because a turtle's heart will beat for hours after he has been cut up and butchered. But the old man thought, I have such a heart too and my feet and hands are like theirs. He ate the white eggs to give himself strength. He ate them all through May to be strong in September and October for the truly big fish.

He also drank a cup of shark liver oil each day from the big drum in the shack where many of the fishermen kept their gear. It was there for all fishermen who wanted it. Most fishermen hated the taste. But it was no worse than getting up at the hours that they rose and it was very good against all colds and grippes* and it was good for the eyes.

Now the old man looked up and saw that the bird was circling again.

---

* **logger-heads** : tropical sea turtles with hard shells and large heads.
* **in their armour-plating** : 「갑옷으로 몸을 감싼」.
* **trunk-backs** : a kind of tropical sea turtle.
* **grippe** [grip] : influenza.

"He's found fish," he said aloud. No flying fish broke the surface and there was no scattering of bait fish. But as the old man watched, a small tuna rose in the air, turned and dropped head first into the water. The tuna shone silver in the sun and after he had dropped back into the water another and another rose and they were jumping in all directions, churning the water and leaping in long jumps after the bait. They were circling it and driving it.

If they don't travel too fast I will get into them, the old man thought, and he watched the school working the water white* and the bird now dropping and dipping into the bait fish that were forced to the surface* in their panic.

"The bird is a great help," the old man said. Just then the stern line came taut* under his foot, where he had kept a loop of the line,* and he dropped his oars and felt the weight of the small tuna's shivering pull as he held the line firm and commenced to haul it in. The shivering increased as he pulled in and he could see the blue back of the fish in the water and the gold of his sides before he swung him over the side* and into

---

* **the school working the water white** :「물거품을 하얗게 일으키고 있는 魚群」.
* **were forced to the surface** :「할 수 없이 水面으로 몰려나온」.
* **came taut** : became taut,「팽팽해졌다」.
* **where he had kept a loop of the line** :「동그랗게 말아서 발로 딛고 있던」.
* **He swung him over the side.** :「뱃전 너머로 획 올려 넘겼다」.

the boat. He lay in the stern in the sun, compact and bullet shaped, his big, unintelligent eyes staring as he thumped his life out against the planking of the boat* with the quick shivering strokes of his neat, fast-moving tail. The old man hit him on the head for kindness and kicked him, his body still shuddering, under the shade of the stern.

"Albacore," he said aloud. "He'll make a beautiful bait. He'll weigh ten pounds."

He did not remember when he had first started to talk aloud when he was by himself.* He had sung when he was by himself in the old days and he had sung at night sometimes when he was alone steering on his watch* in the smacks* or in the turtle boats. He had probably started to talk aloud, when alone, when the boy had left. But he did not remember. When he and the boy fished together they usually spoke only when it was necessary. They talked at night or when they were storm-bound by bad weather. It was considered a virtue not to talk unnecessarily at sea and the old man had always considered it so and respected it. But now he said his thoughts aloud many times since there was no one that they could annoy.

---

* **as he thumped…of the boat** : 「팔딱거리며 제 생명을 배의 나무 바닥에 두들겨 부수면서」.
* **when he was by himself** : 「혼자 있을 때」.
* **on his watch** : 「자기 당번 중에」.
* **smacks** : 물고기를 살게 잡아두는 통발을 실은 魚船.

"If the others heard me talking out loud they would think that I am crazy," he said aloud. "But since I am not crazy, I do not care. And the rich have radios to talk to them in their boats and to bring them the baseball."*

Now is no time to think of baseball, he thought. Now is the time to think of only one thing. That which I was born for. There might be a big one around that school, he thought. I picked up only a straggler from the albacore that were feeding. But they are working*far out and fast. Everything that shows on the surface today travels very fast and to the north-east. Can that be the time of day?*Or is it some sign of weather that I do not know?

He could not see the green of the shore now but only the tops of the blue hills that showed white as though they were snow-capped and the clouds that looked like high snow mountains above them. The sea was very dark and the light made prisms in the water. The myriad flecks of the plankton were annulled now by the high sun and it was only the great deep prisms in the blue water that the old man saw now with his lines going straight down into the water that was a mile deep.

---

* **bring them the baseball**:「야구시합도 방송해주는」.
* **working** : marching.
* **Can that be the time of day?** : be 다음에 for를 보충할 것. 「그것은 時間의 탓일까 ?」

The tuna, the fishermen called all the fish of that species tuna and only distinguished among them by their proper names when they came to sell them or to trade them for baits,* were down again. The sun was hot now and the old man felt it on the back of his neck and felt the sweat trickle down his back as he rowed.

I could just drift,* he thought, and sleep and put a bight of line around my toe to wake me. But today is eighty-five days and I should fish the day well.

Just then, watching his lines, he saw one of the projecting green sticks dip sharply.

"Yes," he said. "Yes," and shipped his oars* without bumping the boat. He reached out for the line and held it softly between the thumb and forefinger of his right hand. He felt no strain nor weight and he held the line lightly. Then it came again. This time it was a tentative pull, not solid nor heavy, and he knew exactly what it was. One hundred fathoms down a marlin was eating the sardines that covered the point and the shank of the hook where the hand-forged hook* projected from the head of the small tuna.

The old man held the line delicately, and softly, with his left hand, unleashed it from the stick. Now he

---

- **trade～for bait** : 「미끼와 교환한다」.
- **I could just drift.** : 「배 가는 대로 떠 있기만 하면 된다」.
- **He shipped his oars.** : 「노를 거두어 노받이에 걸었다」.
- **hand-forged hook** : 「손으로 벼려서 만든 갈고리」.

could let it run through his fingers without the fish feeling any tension.*

This far out,* he must be huge in this month, he thought. Eat them, fish. Eat them. Please eat them. How fresh they are and you down there six hundred feet in that cold water in the dark. Make another turn in the dark and come back and eat them.

He felt the light delicate pulling and then a harder pull when a sardine's head must have been more difficult to break from the hook. Then there was nothing.

"Come on," the old man said aloud. "Make another turn. Just smell them. Aren't they lovely? Eat them good* now and then there is the tuna. Hard and cold and lovely. Don't be shy, fish. Eat them."

He waited with the line between his thumb and his finger, watching it and the other lines at the same time for the fish might have swum up or down. Then came the same delicate pulling touch again.

"He'll take it," the old man said aloud. "God help him to take it."

He did not take it though. He was gone and the old man felt nothing.

---

* **without the fish feeling any tension** : 「고기에게 아무런 힘을 느끼지 않게 하고서」.
* **This far out** : 「이렇게까지 멀리 나왔으니」.
* **Eat them good.** : good : well.

"He can't have gone," he said. "Christ knows* he can't have gone. He's making a turn. Maybe he has been hooked before and he remembers something of it."

Then he felt the gentle touch on the line and he was happy.

"It was only his turn," he said. "He'll take it."

He was happy feeling* the gentle pulling and then he felt something hard and unbelievably heavy. It was the weight of the fish and he let the line slip down, down, down, unrolling off* the first of the two reserve coils. As it went down, slipping lightly through the old man's fingers, he still could feel the great weight, though the pressure of his thumb and finger were almost imperceptible.

"What a fish," he said. "He has it sideways in his mouth now and he is moving off with it."

Then he will turn and swallow it, he thought. He did not say that because he knew that if you said a good thing it might not happen. He knew what a huge fish this was and he thought of him moving away in the darkness with the tuna held crosswise in his mouth.* At that moment he felt him stop moving but

* **Christ knows** : 「神에게 맹세코…이다. 확실히, 아무도 모른다」.
* **feeling** : as he felt～.
* **unrolling off** : 「풀어주면서」.
* **with the tuna held crosswise in his mouth** : 「다랑어를 입에 가로 물고」.

the weight was still there. Then the weight increased and he gave more line. He tightened the pressure of his thumb and finger for a moment and the weight increased and was going straight down.

"He's taken it," he said. "Now I'll let him eat it well."

He let the line slip through his fingers while he reached down with his left hand and made fast the free end of the two reserve coils* to the loop of the two reserve coils of the next line. Now he was ready. He had three forty-fathom coils of line in reserve now, as well as the coil he was using.

"Eat it a little more," he said. "Eat it well."

Eat it so that the point of the hook goes into your heart and kills you, he thought. Come up easy and let me put the harpoon into you. All right. Are you ready? Have you been long enough at table?*

"Now!" he said aloud and struck hard* with both hands, gained* a yard of line and then struck again and again, swinging* with each arm alternately on the cord with all the strength of his arms and the pivoted weight of his body.*

---

* **made fast the free end of the two reserve coils** : 「두 개의 둘둘 말아둔 예비낚시줄의 매어있지 않은 끝을 단단히 매었다」. free : 매어있지 않는.
* **Have you been long enough at table?** : 「이젠 먹을 만큼 먹었나?」.
* **struck hard** : pulled hard.
* **gained** : 「끌어당겼다」.
* **swinging~on the cord** : 「낚시줄을 감아들이면서」.

Nothing happened. The fish just moved away slowly and the old man could not raise him an inch. His line was strong and made for heavy fish and he held it against his back* until it was so taut that beads of water were jumping from it. Then it began to make a slow hissing sound in the water and he still held it, bracing himself against the thwart and leaning back against the pull.* The boat began to move slowly off toward the north-west.

The fish moved steadily and they travelled slowly on the calm water. The other baits were still in the water but there was nothing to be done.

"I wish I had the boy," the old man said aloud. "I'm being towed by a fish and I'm the towing bitt.* I could make the line fast. But then he could break it. I must hold him all I can and give him line when he must have it. Thank God* he is travelling and not going down."

What I will do if he decides to go down,* I don't know. What I'll do if he sounds* and dies I don't know.

---

* **(with) the pivoted weight of his body** : 「全身의 무게에 중심을 두고」
* **He held it against his back.** : 「낚시줄을 등에다 메고 버티었다」.
* **leaning back against the pull** : 「끄는 힘에 맞서 몸을 뒤로 젖히고는」
* **I'm the towing bitt.**: 「나는 말뚝이 된 셈이군」. bitt는 닻이나 밧줄 등을 매어두는 繫柱.
* **Thank God** : 「아, 고마워라. 고맙게도」.
* **He is travelling and not going down.** :「움직이고는 있는데 깊은 곳으로 내려가지는 않는다」.
* **sound** : dive suddenly and deeply.

But I'll do something. There are plenty of things I can do.

He held the line against his back and watched its slant in the water and the skiff moving steadily to the north-west.

This will kill him, the old man thought. He can't do this forever. But four hours later the fish was still swimming steadily out to sea, towing the skiff, and the old man was still braced solidly with the line across his back.

"It was noon when I hooked him," he said. "And I have never seen him."

He had pushed his straw hat hard down on his head before he hooked the fish and it was cutting his forehead.* He was thirsty too and he got down on his knees and, being careful not to jerk on the line,* moved as far into the bow as he could get and reached the water bottle with one hand. He opened it and drank a little. Then he rested against the bow. He rested sitting on the un-stepped mast* and sail and tried not to think but only to endure.

Then he looked behind him and saw that no land was visible. That makes no difference,* he thought. I

---

* **It was cutting his forehead.** :「그것이 이마에 박혀서 이마가 아팠다」.
* **jerk on the line** :「줄을 갑자기 당기다」.
* **unstepped mast** :「台座에서 빼낸 돛대」.
* **That makes no difference.** :「육지가 안 보여도 상관없다」는 뜻.

can always come in on the glow from Havana. There are two more hours before the sun sets and maybe he will come up before that. If he doesn't maybe he will come up with the moon. If he does not do that maybe he will come up with the sunrise. I have no cramps and I feel strong. It is he that has the hook in his mouth. But what a fish to pull like that. He must have his mouth shut tight on the wire. I wish I could see him. I wish I could see him only once to know what I have against me.*

The fish never changed his course nor his direction all that night as far as the man could tell from watching the stars.* It was cold after the sun went down and the old man's sweat dried cold on his back and his arms and his old legs. During the day he had taken the sack that covered the bait box and spread it in the sun to dry. After the sun went down he tied it around his neck so that it hung down over his back and he cautiously worked* it down under the line that was across his shoulders now. The sack cushioned the line* and he had found a way of leaning forward against the bow so that he was almost comfortable. The position actually was only somewhat less intolerable;* but he thought of

* **what I have against me** : 「나에게 저항하고 있는 놈이 무엇인지」.
* **as far as the man could tell from watching the stars** : 「별의 위치로 미루어 판단할 수 있는 한」.
* **worked** : pulled.
* **The sack cushioned the line.**: 「푸대가 낚시줄의 방석노릇을 하였다」.

it as almost comfortable.

I can do nothing with him and he can do nothing with me, he thought. Not as long as he keeps this up.*

Once he stood up and urinated* over the side of the skiff and looked at the stars and checked his course.* The line showed like a phosphorescent streak in the water straight out from his shoulders. They were moving more slowly now and the glow of Havana was not so strong, so that he knew the current must be carrying them to the eastward. If I lose the glare of Havana we must be going more to the eastward, he thought. For if the fish's course held true* I must see it for many more hours. I wonder how the baseball came out* in the grand leagues today, he thought. It would be wonderful to do this with a radio. Then he thought, think of it always. Think of what you are doing. You must do nothing stupid.

Then he said aloud, "I wish I had the boy. To help me and to see this."

No one should be alone in their old age, he thought.

---

* **less intolerable** : 「겨우 견딜 만한」.
* **Not as long as he keeps this up.** : 「저 놈이 이대로 버티고 있는 한 피차가 별도리 없다」 Not : I can do nothing with him and he can do nothing with me.
* **urinate** : 「오줌을 누다」.
* **check his course** : 「進路를 확인하다」.
* **if the fish's course held true** : 「고기가 제 코스를 똑바로 계속하고 있다면」.
* **came out** : 「결과가 나타났다」.

But it is unavoidable. I must remember to eat the tuna before he spoils in order to keep strong. Remember, no matter how little you want to,* that you must eat him in the morning. Remember, he said to himself.

During the night two porpoises came around the boat and he could hear them rolling and blowing. He could tell the difference between the blowing noise the male made and the sighing blow of the female.

"They are good," he said. "They play and make jokes and love one another. They are our brothers like the flying fish."*

Then he began to pity the great fish that he had hooked. He is wonderful and strange and who knows how old he is, he thought. Never have I had such a strong fish nor one who acted so strangely. Perhaps he is too wise to jump. He could ruin me by jumping or by a wild rush. But perhaps he has been hooked many times before and he knows that this is how he should make his fight. He cannot know that it is only one man against him,* nor that it is an old man. But what a great fish he is and what will he bring in the market* if the

---

* **want to** : 다음에 eat를 보충할 것.
* **They are brothers like the flying fish.** : 이 문장은 주인공(즉 Hemingway)이 友愛精神 뿐만 아니라 汎愛精神의 소유자가 되었다는 것을 보여주는 문장이다. 좀 더 자세한 解說을 위해선 拙著 〈研究〉 p. 180을 보라.
* **It is only one man against him.** :「그하고 겨루고 있는 상대가 겨우 하나밖에 없다」.
* **what he will bring in the market** :「시장에다 팔면 굉장한 돈이 될 것이다」.

flesh is good. He took the bait like a male and he pulls like a male and his fight has no panic in it. I wonder if he has any plans or if he is just as desperate as I am?

He remembered the time he had hooked one of a pair of marlin. The male fish always let the female fish feed first and the hooked fish, the female, made a wild, panic-stricken, despairing fight that soon exhausted her, and all the time the male had stayed with her, crossing the line and circling with her on the surface. He had stayed so close that the old man was afraid he would cut the line with his tail which was sharp as a scythe* and almost of that size and shape.* When the old man had gaffed her and clubbed her, holding the rapier bill* with its sandpaper edge and clubbing her across the top of her head until her colour turned to a colour almost like the backing of mirrors, and then, with the boy's aid, hoisted her aboard, the male fish had stayed by the side of the boat. Then, while the old man was clearing the lines* and preparing the harpoon, the male fish jumped high into the air beside the boat to see where the female was and then went down deep, his lavender wings, that were his pectoral fins, spread wide and all his wide lavender stripes showing. He was

* **scythe** [saið] : 「긴 자루가 달린 풀 베는 낫」.
* **of that size and shape** : 「그만한 크기와 그런 모양(낫모양)의」.
* **rapier** [réipiər] **bill** : 「가느다란 쌍날칼처럼 생긴 뾰죽한 주둥이」.
* **clear the line** : 「낚시줄을 정돈하다」.

beautiful, the old man remembered, and he had stayed.

That was the saddest thing I ever saw with them, the old man thought. The boy was sad too and we begged her pardon and butchered her promptly.

"I wish the boy was here," he said aloud and settled himself against the rounded planks of the bow and felt the strength of the great fish through the line he held across his shoulders moving steadily toward whatever he had chosen.

When once, through my treachery,* it had been necessary to him to make a choice, the old man thought.

His choice had been to stay in the deep dark water far out beyond* all snares and traps and treacheries. My choice was to go there to find him beyond all people.* Beyond all people in the world. Now we are joined together and have been since noon. And no one to help either one of us.

Perhaps I should not have been a fisherman, he thought. But that was the thing that I was born for. I must surely remember to eat the tuna after it gets light.

Some time before daylight something took one of the baits that were behind him. He heard the stick break and the line begin to rush out over the gunwale of the skiff. In the darkness he loosened his sheath knife and

* **once, through my treachery** : 「일단 계교에 걸려든 이상」.
* **far out beyond** : 「미치지 못하게 멀리 떨어진」.
* **beyond all people** : 「모든 사람이 미치지 못하는」.

taking all the strain of the fish on his left shoulder he leaned back and cut the line against the wood of the gunwale. Then he cut the other line closest to him and in the dark made the loose ends of the reserve coils fast. He worked skillfully with the one hand and put his foot on the coils to hold them as he drew his knots tight. Now he had six reserve coils of line. There were two from each bait he had severed and the two from the bait the fish had taken and they were all connected.

After it is light, he thought, I will work back to the forty-fathom bait and cut it away too and link up the reserve coils. I will have lost two hundred fathoms of good Catalan *cardel**and the hooks and leaders. That can be replaced. But who replaces this fish if I hook some fish and it cuts him off? I don't know what that fish was that took the bait just now. It could have been a marlin or a broadbill or a shark. I never felt him. I had to get rid of him too fast.

Aloud he said, "I wish I had the boy."

But you haven't got the boy, he thought. You have only yourself and you had better work back to the last line now,* in the dark or not in the dark,* and cut it

---

* ***Catalan cordel***[kǽtalan kordel] :Spain의 Catalonia地方産의 밧줄. cordel : (Sp.) cord.

* **You had better work back to the last line now.**:「이젠 끝줄 있는 대로 돌아가는 것이 좋겠다」. work back : go back.

* **in the dark or not in the dark** :「어둡든 어둡지 않든」.

away and hook up the two reserve coils.

So he did it. It was difficult in the dark and once the fish made a surge that pulled him down on his face and made a cut below his eye. The blood ran down his cheek a little way. But it coagulated and dried before it reached his chin and he worked his way back to the bow* and rested against the wood. He adjusted the sack and carefully worked* the line so that it came across a new part of his shoulders and, holding it anchored* with his shoulders, he carefully felt the pull of the fish and then felt with his hand the progress of the skiff through the water.*

I wonder what he made that lurch for,* he thought. The wire must have slipped* on the great hill of his back. Certainly his back cannot feel as badly as mine does. But he cannot pull this skiff forever, no matter how great he is. Now everything is cleared away that might make trouble* and I have a big reserve of line; all that a man can ask.*

---

* **he worked his way back to the bow** : 「이물 쪽으로 돌아갔다」.
* **worked** : 「옮겼다」.
* **anchored** : fixed.
* **through the water** : 「물 속에 손을 담가」.
* **what he made that lurch for** : 「무엇 때문에 저놈이 저렇게 꿈틀거렸는지」. that lurch : lurch like that, that는 副詞.
* **slipped** : rubbed.
* **now everything is cleared away that might make trouble** : 「나중에 말썽거리가 될 만한 것은 다 치워버렸다」. that 의 先行詞는 everything.
* **all that a man can ask** : I have all that a man can ask.「이 이상 바랄게 없다」.

"Fish," he said softly, aloud, "I'll stay with you until I am dead."

He'll stay with me too, I suppose, the old man thought and he waited for it to be light. It was cold now in the time before daylight and he pushed* against the wood to be warm. I can do it as long as he can, he thought. And in the first light* the line extended out and down into the water. The boat moved steadily and when the first edge of the sun rose it was on the old man's right shoulder.

"He's headed north," the old man said. The current will have set us far to the eastward, he thought. I wish he would turn with the current. That would show that he was tiring.

When the sun had risen further the old man realized that the fish was not tiring. There was only one favorable sign. The slant of the line showed he was swimming at a lesser depth. That did not necessarily mean that he would jump. But he might.

"God let him jump," the old man said. "I have enough line to handle him."

Maybe if I can increase the tension just a little it will hurt him and he will jump, he thought. Now that it is daylight let him jump so that he'll fill the sacks along his backbone with air and then he cannot go

* **push** : 「비벼대다」.
* **first light** : 「여명」.

deep to die.

He tried to increase the tension, but the line had been taut up to the very edge of the breaking point since he had hooked the fish and he felt the harshness as he leaned back to pull and knew he could put no more strain on it. I must not jerk it ever, he thought. Each jerk widens the cut the hook makes and then when he does jump he might throw it. Anyway I feel better with the sun and for once* I do not have to look into it.

There was yellow weed on the line but the old man knew that only made an added drag and he was pleased. It was the yellow Gulf weed that had made so much phosphorescence in the night.

"Fish," he said, "I love you and respect you very much. But I will kill you dead before this day ends."

Let us hope so, he thought.

A small bird came toward the skiff from the north. He was a warbler and flying very low over the water. The old man could see that he was very tired.

The bird made* the stern of the boat and rested there. Then he flew around the old man's head and rested on the line where he was more comfortable.

"How old are you?" the old man asked the bird. "Is this your first trip?"

---

* **for once** : 「이번만큼은」.
* **made** : reached.

The bird looked at him when he spoke. He was too tired even to examine the line and he teetered on it as his delicate feet gripped it fast.

"It's steady," the old man told him. "It's too steady. You shouldn't be that tired* after a windless night.* What are birds coming to?*"

The hawks, he thought, that come out to sea to meet them. But he said nothing of this to the bird who could not understand him anyway and who would learn about the hawks soon enough.

"Take a good rest, small bird," he said. "Then go in and take your chance like any man or bird or fish."

It encouraged him to talk* because his back had stiffened in the night and it hurt truly now.

"Stay at my house if you like, bird," he said. "I am sorry I cannot hoist the sail and take you in* with the small breeze that is rising. But I am with a friend."

Just then the fish gave a sudden lurch that pulled the old man down onto the bow and would have pulled him overboard if he had not braced himself and given some line.

---

* **that tired** : tired like that. that는 副詞.
* **after a windless night** :「간밤엔 바람도 없었는데」.
* **What are birds coming to?** :「새들은 과연 앞으로 어떻게 되는 것일까?」.
* **It encouraged him to talk.** :「이렇게 얘기를 하고 보니 기분이 좋아지는 것만 같았다」.
* **take you in** :「너를 육지로 데려다주다」.

The bird had flown up when the line jerked and the old man had not even seen him go. He felt the line carefully with his right hand and noticed his hand was bleeding.

"Something hurt him then," he said aloud and pulled back on the line to see if he could turn the fish. But when he was touching the breaking point he held steady and settled back against the strain of the line.

"You're feeling it now, fish," he said. "And so, God knows, am I."

He looked around for the bird now because he would have liked him for company.* The bird was gone.

You did not stay long, the man thought. But it is rougher where you are going until you make the shore.* How did I let the fish cut me with that one quick pull he made? I must be getting very stupid. Or perhaps I was looking at the small bird and thinking of him. Now I will pay attention to my work and then I must eat the tuna so that I will not have a failure of strength.

"I wish the boy were here and that I had some salt," he said aloud.

Shifting the weight of the line to his left shoulder and kneeling carefully he washed his hand in the ocean and held it there, submerged,* for more than a

* **for company** : 「동무로」.
* **make the shore** : reach the shore.
* **submerged** : 「물속에 잠긴채」. held의 補語.

minute watching the blood trail away and the steady movement of the water against his hand as the boat moved.

"He has slowed much," he said.

The old man would have liked to keep his hand in the salt water longer but he was afraid of another sudden lurch by the fish and he stood up and braced himself and held his hand up against the sun. It was only a line burn* that had cut his flesh. But it was in the working part of his hand. He knew he would need his hands before this was over and he did not like to be cut before it started.

"Now," he said, when his hand had dried, "I must eat the small tuna. I can reach him with the gaff and eat him here in comfort."

He knelt down and found the tuna under the stern with the gaff and drew it toward him keeping it clear of the coiled lines.* Holding the line with his left shoulder again, and bracing on his left hand and arm, he took the tuna off the gaff hook and put the gaff back in place. He put one knee on the fish and cut strips of dark red meat longitudinally from the back of the head to the tail. They were wedge-shaped strips and he cut

---

* **line burn** : 「낚시줄에 스쳐서 벗겨진 상처」.
* **keeping it clear of the coiled lines** : 「둘둘 사린 줄에 닿지 않도록 그것을 멀리 두면서」. it : tuna.

them from next to the back bone down to the edge of the belly.* When he had cut six strips he spread them out on the wood of the bow, wiped his knife on his trousers, and lifted the carcass of the bonito by the tail and dropped it overboard.

"I don't think I can eat an entire one," he said and drew his knife across one of the strips. He could feel the steady hard pull of the line and his left hand was cramped. It drew up tight* on the heavy cord and he looked at it in disgust.*

"What kind of a hand is that," he said. "Cramp then if you want. Make yourself into a claw.* It will do you no good."*

Come on, he thought and looked down into the dark water at the slant of the line. Eat it now and it will strengthen the hand. It is not the hand's fault and you have been many hours with the fish. But you can stay with him forever. Eat the bonito now.

He picked up a piece and put it in his mouth and chewed it slowly. It was not unpleasant.

Chew it well, he thought, and get all the juices. It would not be bad to eat with a little lime or with

---

* **from next to the back bone down to the edge of the belly** : 「등뼈 가장 가까운 데로부터 배밑까지」. next : nearest.
* **It drew up tight.** : 「손이 빳빳하게 오그라들었다」.
* **in disgust** : 「화가 나서」.
* **Make yourself into a claw.** : 「매의 발톱처럼 오그라들어라」.
* **It will do you no good.** : 「그래봤자 별거 없을 게다」. good : use, advantage.

lemon or with salt.

"How do you feel, hand?" he asked the cramped hand that was almost as stiff as rigor mortis.* "I'll eat some more for you."

He ate the other part of the piece that he had cut in two. He chewed it carefully and then spat out the skin.

"How does it go, hand?* Or is it too early to know?"

He took another full piece and chewed it.

"It is a strong full-blooded fish," he thought. "I was lucky to get him instead of dolphin. Dolphin is too sweet. This is hardly sweet at all and all the strength* is still in it."

There is no sense in being anything but practical though, he thought.* I wish I had some salt. And I do not know whether the sun will rot or dry what is left, so I had better eat it all although I am not hungry. The fish is calm and steady. I will eat it all and then I will be ready.

"Be patient, hand," he said. "I do this for you."

I wish I could feed the fish, he thought. He is my brother.* But I must kill him and keep strong to do it.

* **rigor mortis** : 「死后硬直」.
* **How does it go, hand?** : 「손아 좀 어떠냐？」.
* **strength** : 「탄탄한 느낌」.
* **There is no sense in being anything but practical though, he thought.** : 「그렇기는 하지만 실질적인 생각 말고는 무엇이든 무의미한 것이지 하고 그는 생각했다」.
* **I wish I could feed the fish, he thought. He is my brother** : 주인공을 통해 Hemingway의 汎愛思想이 나타난 好例의 문장이다.

Slowly and conscientiously he ate all of the wedge-shaped strips of fish.

He straightened up, wiping his hand on his trousers.

"Now," he said. "You can let the cord go, hand,* and I will handle him with the right arm alone until you stop that nonsense." He put his left foot on the heavy line that the left hand had held and lay back against the pull against his back.*

"God help me to have the cramp go," he said. "Because I do not know what the fish is going to do."

But he seems calm, he thought, and following his plan. But what is his plan, he thought. And what is mine? Mine I must improvise to his because of his great size. If he will jump I can kill him. But he stays down forever. Then I will stay down with him forever.

He rubbed the cramped hand against his trousers and tried to gentle the fingers. But it would not open. Maybe it will open with the sun, he thought. Maybe it will open when the strong raw tuna is digested. If I have to have it, I will open it, cost whatever it costs.* But I do not want to open it now by force. Let it open by itself and come back of its own accord.* After all I

---

* **You can let the cord go, hand.** : 「손아, 이젠 줄을 놔도 좋다」. let go release, set at liberty. 「해방하다」.
* **lay back against the pull against his back** : 「등을 조이며 당겨드는 줄에 기대고 누웠다」.
* **cost whatever it cost** : 「무슨 짓(댓가)을 해서(지불해서)라도」.
* **of its own accord** : 「저절로, 제 마음대로」.

abused it much in the night when it was necessary to free* and untie the various lines.

He looked across the sea and knew how alone he was now. But he could see the prisms in the deep dark water and the line stretching ahead and the strange undulation of the calm.* The clouds were building up now for the trade wind* and he looked ahead and saw a flight of wild ducks etching themselves against the sky over the water, then blurring, then etching again and he knew no man was ever alone on the sea.

He thought of how some men feared being out of sight of land in a small boat and knew they were right in the months of sudden bad weather. But now they were in hurricane months and, when there are no hurricanes, the weather of hurricane months is the best of all the year.

If there is a hurricane you always see the signs of it in the sky for days ahead, if you are at sea. They do not see it ashore because they do not know what to look for, he thought. The land must make a difference too, in the shape of the clouds.* But we have no hurricane coming now.

---

* **free** : 「풀어주다」.
* **the calm** : the calm sea.
* **for the trade wind** : 「무역풍 때문에」.
* **etching themselves against the sky** : 「하늘을 배경으로 하여 뚜렷한 자태를 나타냈다가는」.
* **The land...in the shape of the clouds.** : 「역시 육지 자체가 구름의 형태를 바꿔놓는 것임에 틀림없다」.

He looked at the sky and saw the white cumulus* built like friendly piles of ice cream and high above were the thin feathers of the cirrus* against the high September sky.

"Light *brisa*,*" he said. "Better weather for me than for you, fish."

His left hand was still cramped, but he was unknotting it slowly.

I hate a cramp, he thought. It is a treachery of one's own body. It is humiliating before others to have a diarrhoea* from ptomaine poisoning or to vomit from it. But a cramp, he thought of it as a *calambre*,* humiliates oneself especially when one is alone.

If the boy were here he could rub it for me and loosen it down from the forearm, he thought. But it will loosen up.*

Then, with his right hand he felt the difference in the pull of the line before he saw the slant change in the water. Then, as he leaned against the line and slapped his left hand hard and fast against his thigh he saw the line slanting slowly upward.

"He's coming up," he said. "Come on hand.* Please

* **cumulus** [kjú:mjuləs] :「송이구름」.
* **cirrus** [sírəs] :「巻雲」.
* **brisa** [brisa] :(Sp.) breeze.
* **diarrhoea** [dáiərí(:)ə] :「설사」.
* ***calambre*** [kalambre] : (Sp.) cramp.
* **loosen up** :「풀리다」.
* **come on hand** :「가까이 오너라」. hand (adv.) : close, near

come on."

The line rose slowly and steadily and then the surface of the ocean bulged ahead of the boat and the fish came out. He came out unendingly and water poured from his sides. He was bright in the sun and his head and back were dark purple and in the sun the stripes on his sides showed wide and a light lavender. His sword* was as long as a baseball bat and tapered like a rapier and he rose his full length from the water and then re-entered it, smoothly, like a diver and the old man saw the great scythe-blade of his tail go under and the line commenced to race out.*

"He is two feet longer than the skiff," the old man said. The line was going out fast but steadily and the fish was not panicked. The old man was trying with both hands to keep the line just inside of breaking strength.* He knew that if he could not slow the fish with a steady pressure the fish could take out all the line and break it.

He is a great fish and I must convince him,* he thought. I must never let him learn his strength nor what he could do if he made his run.* If I were him I

---

* **sword** : 「劍같은 뾰족한 부리」.
* **race out** : 「풀려나가다」.
* **inside of breaking strength** : 「끊어지지 않을 정도로」.
* **I must convince him** : 「깨닫게 해야만 한다」. convince : 확신시키다, 납득시키다. *cf.* convince oneself of : …을 확신하다.
* **if he made his run** : 「도망친다면」.

would put in everything now and go* until something broke.* But, thank God, they are not as intelligent as we who kill them; although they are more noble and more able.

The old man had seen many great fish. He had seen many that weighed more than a thousand pounds and he had caught two of that size in his life, but never alone. Now alone, and out of sight of land, he was fast* to the biggest fish that he had ever seen and bigger than he had ever heard of, and his left hand was still as tight as the gripped claws of an eagle.

It will uncramp though, he thought. Surely it will uncramp to help my right hand. There are three things that are brothers: the fish and my two hands. It must uncramp. It is unworthy of it to be cramped. The fish had slowed again and was going at his usual pace.

I wonder why he jumped, the old man thought. He jumped almost as though to show me how big he was. I know now, anyway, he thought. I wish I could show him what sort of man I am. But then he would see the cramped hand. Let him think I am more man than I am and I will be so. I wish I was the fish, he thought, with everything he has against only my will and my intelligence.

---

* **I would put in everything now and go.** : 「있는 수단을 다해서 무슨 요절이 날 때까지 해보겠다」.
* **until something broke** : 「무슨 일이 일어날 때까지」.
* **was fast** : was firmly attached.

He settled comfortably against the wood and took his suffering as it came and the fish swam steadily and the boat moved slowly through the dark water. There was a small sea rising with the wind coming up from the east and at noon the old man's left hand was uncramped.

"Bad news for you, fish," he said and shifted the line over the sacks that covered his shoulders.

He was comfortable but suffering, although he did not admit the suffering at all.

"I am not religious*," he said. "But I will say ten Our Fathers and ten Hail Marys* that I should catch* this fish, and I promise to make a pilgrimage to the Virgin of Cobre if I catch him. That is a promise."

He commenced to say his prayers mechanically. Sometimes he would be so tired that he could not remember the prayer and then he would say them fast so

---

* **I am not religious.** : 주인공을 통해 작가의 無神論이 나타난 好例의 문장이다. Hemingway에게는 초기의 작품부터 최종작에 이르기까지 일관된 無神論的 思想을 갖고 있다. 특히, Hemingway가 宗教的인 作家이냐를 이 作品을 중심으로 하여 고찰할 때, 主人公의 宗教性이 그 本質에 있어서는 다른 作品의 主人公과 마찬가지로 "I am not religious." 이기는 하지만, 이 作品에서는 유독 Christian symbolism이 강하게 그 냄새를 풍기고 있다. 사실 이 作品만큼 이와 병행하여 humanism이 강조되어 있는 作品도 없다. 이 문제에 관하여서는 다음 論文을 參照하라.

Baker의 前揭書와 Joseph Waldmeir, "Confiteor Hominem: Ernest Hemingway's Religion of Man," *Hemingway*, ed. Robert P Weeks, 1962, pp. 161 – 171; 拙著 〈研究〉 pp. 228 – 239.

* **Say ten our Fathers and ten Hail Marys.** :「"Our Father who art in Heaven"으로 시작하는 천주경과 p. 504, l. 3에 나오는 "Hail Mary full of Grace"로 시작되는 성모경을 열번이라도 외우겠다」.

* **that I should catch** : that I might catch,「잡을 수 있도록」.

that they would come automatically. Hail Marys are easier to say than Our Fathers, he thought.

"Hail Mary full of Grace the Lord is with thee. Blessed art thou among women and blessed is the fruit of thy womb, Jesus. Holy Mary, Mother of God, pray for us sinners now and at the hour of our death. Amen." Then he added, "Blessed Virgin, pray for the death of this fish. Wonderful though he is."

With his prayers said,* and feeling much better, but suffering exactly as much, and perhaps a little more,* he leaned against the wood of the bow* and began, mechan-

---

* **with his prayers said** :「기도를 올리고 나니」.
* **feeling much better...a little more** :「기분은 훨씬 나아진 것 같았으나 고통은 여전했고, 어떻게 보면 더해진 것도 같았다」.
* **the wood of the bow** : 도처에서 보이는 wood는 무슨 뜻을 가지고 있나? 이 wood는 예수가 등에 짊어진 十字架의 wood와 동일한 symbol이라고 Backman教授도 Baker教授도 동일하게 논하고 있다. skiff의 wood of the bow를 굳게 딛고 버티는 모습이나, marlin이 몹시 끌어당길 때 등에 스며드는 cord의 중력에 눌려 고민하는 노인의 image는 十字架의 重压에 눌린 예수의 그것과 동일하다는 것이다. 또 하나 "*Ay*", he said loud. "There is no translation for this word and perhaps it is just a noise such as a man might make, involuntarily, feeling the nail go through his hands and into the wood."(p.)이 絶叫는 예수가 十字架에 못박힐 때에 부르짖는 것과 동일하다는 것. 이 밖에 또 그의 방의 벽에 Sacred Heart of Jesus와 Virgin of Cobre의 像이 걸려 있다고 해서 Santiago의 宗教性을 인정하고 동시에 Hemingway를 宗教的인 作家라고 해서는 안된다. 여러 学者들은 그 반대의 견해를 가지고 있다. 오히려 Christian symbolism으로 이 作家가 humanism을 강조하고 있다는 것이다. 아까 든 Joseph Waldmeir, Carlos Baker, Melvin Backman등 諸教授의 見解도 동일하고, 이 문제를 가장 銳利하게 다룬 学者는 John Killinger 教授이다. Killinger 教授는 Hemingway에게는 神은 죽었다고 論하고 있다. 同教授의 著 *Hemingway and the Dead Gods: A Study in Existentialism,* 1960, "Chapter Four, The Death of the Gods" 参照.

ically, to work the fingers* of his left hand.

The sun was hot now although the breeze was rising gently.

"I had better re-bait that little line out over the stern," he said. "If the fish decides to stay another night I will need to eat again and the water is low in the bottle. I don't think I can get anything but a dolphin here. But if I eat him fresh enough he won't be bad. I wish a flying fish would come on board tonight. But I have no light to attract them. A flying fish is excellent to eat raw* and I would not have to cut him up. I must save all my strength now. Christ,* I did not know he was so big."

"I'll kill him though," he said. "In all his greatness and his glory."

Although it is unjust, he thought. But I will show him what a man can do and what a man endures.

"I told the boy I was a strange old man," he said. "Now is when I must prove it."

The thousand times that he had proved it meant nothing. Now he was proving it again. Each time was a new time and he never thought about the past when he was doing it.

I wish he'd sleep and I could sleep and dream about

---

* **work the fingers** : move the fingers.
* **eat raw** : 「날 것으로 먹다」.
* **Christ** : 제기랄, 놀랐을 때나 노했을 때의 감탄사.

the lions, he thought. Why are the lions the main thing that is left?* Don't think, old man, he said to himself. Rest gently now against the wood and think of nothing. He is working.* Work as little as you can.

It was getting into the afternoon and the boat still moved slowly and steadily. But there was an added drag now from the easterly breeze* and the old man rode gently with the small sea* and the hurt of the cord across his back came to him easily and smoothly.

Once in the afternoon the line started to rise again. But the fish only continued to swim at a slightly higher level. The sun was on the old man's left arm and shoulder and on his back. So he knew the fish had turned east of north.*

Now that he had seen him once, he could picture the fish swimming in the water with his purple pectoral fins set wide as wings and the great erect tail slicing through the dark. I wonder how much he sees at that depth, the old man thought. His eye is huge and a horse, with much less eye, can see in the dark. Once I could see quite well in the dark. Not in the absolute

---

- **Why are the lions the main thing that is left?** :「왜 사자만이 자꾸만 머리에 떠오르는 것일까?」.
- **He is working.**: He is moving.
- **There was an added drag from the easterly freeze.** :「동쪽에서 산들바람이 불어와서 고기에게 좀 더 부담을 주었다」.
- **rode gently with the small sea** :「잔잔한 파도를 헤치며 서서히 저어나갔다」.
- **turned east of north**에서 of : from.

dark. But almost as a cat sees.

The sun and his steady movement of his fingers had uncramped his left hand now completely and he began to shift more of the strain to it and he shrugged the muscles of his back to shift the hurt of the cord a little.

"If you're not tired, fish," he said aloud, "you must be very strange."

He felt very tired now and he knew the night would come soon and he tried to think of other things. He thought of the Big Leagues,* to him they were the *Gran Ligas*,* and he knew that the Yankees of New York were playing the *Tigres** of Detroit.

This is the second day now that I do not know the result of the *juegos*,* he thought. But I must have confidence and I must be worthy of the great DiMaggio who does all things perfectly even with the pain of the bone spur in his heel.* What is a bone spur?* he asked himself. *Un espuela de hueso*.* We do not have

---

* **Big Leagues** : National League and the American League.
* ***Gran Ligas***[grɑ:n li:gas] :(Sp.) Big Leagues.
* ***tigres*** [ti:gres] :(Sp.) tigers.
* ***juegos***[huegos] :(Sp.) game.
* **I must be worthy of… in his heel.** : 이 문장은, DiMaggio가 노인에게 금욕주의자로 여겨지고 있음을 보여주며, 따라서 DiMaggio가 giver of strength and vitality의 symbol로 표현되어 있음과, 또한 bone spur가 노인에게 stoicism을 예상케 하는 상징적 의미까지 내포하고 있음을 시사해 주고 있다.
* **bone spur** : painful growth on the bone.
* ***Un espuela de hueso***[un espuéla de uéso] :(Sp.) a spur of bone, bone spur.

them. Can it be as painful as the spur of a fighting cock in one's heel? I do not think I could endure that or the loss of the eye and of both eyes and continue to fight as the fighting cocks do. Man is not much beside* the great birds and beasts. Still I would rather be that beast down there in the darkness of the sea.

"Unless sharks come," he said aloud. "If sharks come, God pity him and me."

Do you believe the great DiMaggio would stay with a fish as long as I will stay with this one? he thought. I am sure he would and more since he is young and strong. Also his father was a fisherman. But would the bone spur hurt him too much?

"I do not know," he said aloud. "I never had a bone spur."

As the sun set he remembered, to give himself more confidence, the time in the tavern at Casablanca* when he had played the hand game with the great negro from Cienfuegos* who was the strongest man on the docks. They had gone* one day and one night with their elbows on a chalk line on the table and their forearms straight up and their hands gripped tight. Each one was trying to force the other's hand down onto the

---

* **Man is not much beside** ～ : 「～에 비하면 인간이란 아무것도 아니다」. beside : compared with.
* **Casablanca** : 仏領 모로코에 있는 대서양 연안의 항구도시.
* **Cienfuegos** : a seaport on the south coast of Cuba.
* **They had gone** : 「두 사람은 버티었다」.

table. There was much betting and people went in and out of the room under the kerosene lights and he had looked at the arm and hand of the negro and at the negro's face. They changed the referees every four hours after the first eight so that the referees could sleep. Blood came out from under the fingernails of both his and the negro's hands and they looked each other in the eye and at their hands and forearms and the bettors went in and out of the room and sat on high chairs against the wall and watched. The walls were painted bright blue and were of wood and the lamps threw their shadows against them. The negro's shadow was huge and it moved on the wall as the breeze moved the lamps.

The odds would change back and forth* all night and they fed the negro rum and lighted cigarettes for him. Then the negro, after the rum, would try for a tremendous effort and once he had the old man, who was not an old man then but was Santiago *El Campeón*,* nearly three inches off balance.* But the old man had raised his hand up to dead even* again. He was sure then that he had the negro, who was a fine man and a great athlete, beaten.* And at daylight when the bettors were

---

* **The odds would change back and forth.** :「勝負는 이편 저편으로 왔다갔다 하였다」.
* **Santiago *El Campeón (sp.)*** : Santiago the champion.
* **three inches off balance** :「3 인치나 이쪽으로 기울었다」.
* **to dead even** :「꼭 맞서게」.
* **had the negro…beaten** :「그 黑人을 이겨냈다」.

asking that it be called a draw* and the referee was shaking his head, he had unleashed his effort and forced the hand of the negro down and down until it rested on the wood. The match had started on a Sunday morning and ended on a Monday morning. Many of the bettors had asked for a draw because they had to go to work on the docks loading sacks of sugar or at the Havana Coal Company. Otherwise everyone would have wanted it to go to a finish. But he had finished it anyway and before anyone had to go to work.

For a long time after that everyone had called him The Champion and there had been a return match in the spring. But not much money was bet and he had won it quite easily since he had broken the confidence of the negro from Cienfuegos in the first match. After that he had a few matches and then no more. He decided that he could beat anyone if he wanted to badly enough* and he decided that it was bad for his right hand for fishing. He had tried a few practice matches with his left hand. But his left hand had always been a traitor and would not do what he called on it to do and he did not trust it.

The sun will bake it out well* now, he thought. It

---

* **a draw** : 「비긴 시합, 피장파장」.
* **if he wanted to badly enough** : to 다음에 beat를 보충. badly : very much.
* **bake it out well** : 「손을 따뜻하게 하여 경련을 없애다」.

should not cramp on me again unless it gets too cold in the night. I wonder what this night will bring.

An airplane passed overhead on its course to Miami* and he watched its shadow scaring up the schools of flying fish.

"With so much flying fish* there should be dolphin," he said, and leaned back* on the line to see if it was possible to gain any* on his fish*. But he could not and it stayed at the hardness and water-drop shivering that preceded breaking*. The boat moved ahead slowly and he watched the airplane until he could no longer see it.

It must be very strange in an airplane, he thought. I wonder what the sea looks like from that height? They should be able to see the fish well if they do not fly too high. I would like to fly very slowly at two hundred fathoms high and see the fish from above. In the turtle boats I was in the cross-trees* of the mast-head and even at that height I saw much. The dolphin look greener from there and you can see their stripes and their purple spots and you can see all of the school as they

---

* **Miami** [maiǽmi] : 미국 Florida주 남동부의 유명한 피한지.
* **with so much flying fish** :「날치가 이렇게 많으니」.
* **gain any** : gain any line.
* **leaned back on the line** :「몸을 뒤로 젖히며 줄을 당겼다」.
* **if it was possible to gain any on his fish** :「고기가 걸린 줄을 조금이라도 끌어 당길 수 있는지」. gain any : gain any line.
* **it stayed ... breaking** :「낚시줄은 금방이라도 끊어질듯 물방울을 튕기며 팽팽해졌다」. hardness : tension.
* **cross-trees** :「기름대」.

swim. Why is it that all the fast-moving fish of the dark current have purple backs and usually purple stripes or spots? The dolphin looks green of course because he is really golden. But when he comes to feed, truly hungry, purple stripes show on his sides as on a marlin. Can it be anger,* or the greater speed he makes that brings them out?

Just before it was dark, as they passed a great island of Sargasso weed that heaved and swung in the light sea as though the ocean were making love with something under a yellow blanket, his small line was taken by a dolphin. He saw it first when it jumped in the air, true gold in the last of the sun and bending and flapping wildly in the air. It jumped again and again in the acrobatics of its fear and he worked his way back to the stern and crouching and holding the big line with his right hand and arm, he pulled the dolphin in with his left hand, stepping on the gained line* each time with his bare left foot. When the fish was at the stern, plunging and cutting* from side to side in desperation, the old man leaned over the stern and lifted the burnished gold fish with its purple spots over the stern. Its jaws were working convulsively in quick bites against the hook* and it pounded the bottom of the skiff with

---

* **Can it be anger?** : Can it be for anger ?
* **gained line** : 「끌어당긴 낚시줄」.
* **plunging and cutting** : 「이리저리 마구 몸부림치면서」.
* **in quick bites against the hook** : 「턱으로 물어서 성급하게 낚시줄을 끊으려고」.

its long flat body, its tail and its head until he clubbed it across the shining golden head until it shivered and was still.

The old man unhooked the fish, re-baited the line with another sardine and tossed it over. Then he worked his way* slowly back to the bow. He washed his left hand and wiped it on his trousers. Then he shifted the heavy line from his right hand to his left and washed his right hand in the sea while he watched the sun go into the ocean and the slant of the big cord.

"He hasn't changed at all," he said. But watching the movement of the water against his hand he noted that it was perceptibly slower.

"I'll lash the two oars together across the stern and that will slow him in the night," he said. "He's good for the night* and so am I."

It would be better to gut the dolphin a little later to save the blood in the meat, he thought. I can do that a little later and lash the oars to make a drag* at the same time. I had better keep the fish quiet now and not disturb him too much at sunset. The setting of the sun is a difficult time for all fish.

He let his hand dry in the air then grasped the line with it and eased himself as much as he could and al-

* **worked his way** : walked.
* **He's good for the night.** : 「오늘밤은 끄덕없다」. good : enough.
* **to make drag** : 「고기에게 부담을 주려고」.

lowed himself to be pulled forward against the wood* so that the boat took the strain as much, or more, than he did.*

I'm learning how to do it, he thought. This part of it anyway.* Then too, remember he hasn't eaten since he took the bait and he is huge and needs much food. I have eaten the whole bonito. Tomorrow I will eat the dolphin. He called it *dorado*.* Perhaps I should eat some of it when I clean it. It will be harder to eat than the bonito. But, then, nothing is easy.

"How do you feel, fish?" he asked aloud. "I feel good and my left hand is better and I have food for a night and a day. Pull the boat, fish."

He did not truly feel good because the pain from the cord across his back had almost passed pain and gone into a dullness that he mistrusted. But I have had worse things than that, he thought. My hand is only cut a little and the cramp is gone from the other. My legs are all right. Also now I have gained on him* in the question of sustenance.*

It was dark now as it becomes dark quickly after the

---

* **against the wood** : 「뱃전에 기대어」.
* **so that the boat ... than he did** : 「그가 힘을 받은 것 만큼, 아니 그 이상 더 보우트가 힘을 반도록」. he did: he took the strain.
* **This part of it anyway** : 「어쨌든 이런 경우에 써 먹는 요령 말이다」.
* ***dorado***[dorado] : (Sp.) dolphin .
* **gain on him** : 「그보다 우세하다」.
* **sustenance** : 「식량」.

sun sets in September. He lay against the worn wood of the bow and rested all that he could. The first stars were out. He did not know the name of Rigel* but he saw it and knew soon they would all be out and he would have all his distant friends.

"The fish is my friend too," he said aloud. "I have never seen or heard of such a fish. But I must kill him. I am glad we do not have to try to kill the stars."

Imagine if each day a man must try to kill the moon, he thought. The moon runs away. But imagine if a man each day should have to try to kill the sun? We were born lucky, he thought.

Then he was sorry for the great fish that had nothing to eat and his determination to kill him never relaxed in his sorrow for him. How many people will he feed, he thought. But are they worthy to eat him? No, of course not. There is no one worthy of eating him from the manner of his behaviour and his great dignity.

I do not understand these things, he thought. But it is good that we do not have to try to kill the sun or the moon or the stars. It is enough to live on the sea and kill our true brothers.

Now, he thought, I must think about the drag. It has its perils and its merits.* I may lose so much line

---

* **Rigel** [raidʒel] : Orion星座의 β 星(이 성좌에서 가장 밝다.)
* **It has its perils and its merits.** : 「一長一短이 있다」.

that* I will lose him, if he makes his effort and the drag made by the oars is in place* and the boat loses all her lightness.* Her lightness prolongs both our suffering but it is my safety since he has great speed that he has never yet employed. No matter what passes* I must gut the dolphin so he does not spoil* and eat some of him to be strong.

Now I will rest an hour more and feel that he is solid and steady before I move back to the stern to do the work and make the decision. In the meantime I can see how he acts and if he shows any changes. The oars are a good trick,* but it has reached the time to play for safety.* He is much fish* still and I saw that the hook was in the corner of his mouth and he has kept his mouth tight shut. The punishment* of the hook is nothing.* The punishment of hunger, and that he is against something* that he does not comprehend, is

---

* **I may lose so much line that** : 「그 만큼 낚시줄을 풀어주게 될 지도 모르기 때문에」.
* **is in place** : 「그대로 있다」.
* **The boat loses all her lightness.** : 「보우트가 무거워지다」.
* **passes** : happens.
* **so** (that) **he does not spoil** : 「상하지 않도록」. he = dolphin.
* **The oars are a good trick.**: That I have lashed the two oars together across the stern is a good trick.
* **the time to play for safety** : 「안전을 기해야 할 때」.
* **He is much fish.** : He is a great fish.
* **punishment** : difficulty.
* **nothing** : unimportant thing.
* **that he is against something** : 「어떤 사태에 맞부딪치고 있다는 것」.

everything.* Rest now, old man, and let him work until your next duty comes.

He rested for what he believed to be two hours. The moon did not rise now until late and he had no way of judging the time. Nor was he really resting except comparatively.* He was still bearing the pull of the fish across his shoulders but he placed his left hand on the gunwale of the bow and confided more and more of the resistance to the fish to the skiff itself.

How simple it would be if I could make the line fast, he thought. But with one small lurch he could break it. I must cushion* the pull of the line with my body and at all times be ready to give line with both hands.

"But you have not slept yet, old man," he said aloud. "It is half a day and a night and now another day and you have not slept. You must devise a way so that you sleep a little if he is quiet and steady. If you do not sleep you might become unclear in the head."

I'm clear enough in the head, he thought. Too clear. I am as clear as the stars that are my brothers. Still I must sleep. They sleep and the moon and the sun sleep and even the ocean sleeps sometimes on certain days when there is no current and a flat calm.

---

* **everything** : the most important thing.
* **Nor was he really resting except comparatively.** : 「앞서 보다는 비교적 휴식을 가졌지만, 정말로 휴식을 취한 것은 아니었다」.
* **cushion** : 「조절하다」.

But remember to sleep, he thought. Make yourself do it and devise some simple and sure way about the lines. Now go back and prepare the dolphin.* It is too dangerous to rig the oars as a drag if you must sleep.

I could go without sleeping, he told himself. But it would be too dangerous.

He started to work his way back to the stern on his hands and knees, being careful not to jerk against the fish. He may be half asleep himself, he thought. But I do not want him to rest. He must pull until he dies.

Back* in the stern he turned so that his left hand held the strain of the line across his shoulders and drew his knife from its sheath with his right hand. The stars were bright now and he saw the dolphin clearly and he pushed the blade of his knife into his head and drew him out from under the stern. He put one of his feet on the fish and slit him quickly from the vent up to the tip of his lower jaw. Then he put his knife down and gutted him with his right hand, scooping him clean and pulling the gills clear. He felt the maw heavy and slippery in his hands and he slit it open. There were two flying fish inside. They were fresh and hard and he laid them side by side and dropped the guts and the gills over the stern. They sank leaving a trail of phosphorescence in the water.

* **prepare the dolphin** : prepare the dolphin to eat.
* **back** : 앞에 Being을 보충할 것.

The dolphin was cold and a leprous gray-white* now in the starlight and the old man skinned one side of him while he held his right foot on the fish's head. Then he turned him over and skinned the other side and cut each side off from the head down to the tail.

He slid the carcass overboard and looked to see if there was any swirl in the water. But there was only the light of its slow descent. He turned then and placed the two flying fish inside the two fillets of fish and putting his knife back in its sheath, he worked his way slowly back to the bow. His back was bent with the weight of the line across it and he carried the fish in his right hand.

Back* in the bow he laid the two fillets of fish out on the wood with the flying fish beside them. After that he settled the line across his shoulders in a new place and held it again with his left hand resting on the gunwale. Then he leaned over the side and washed the flying fish in the water, noting the speed of the water against his hand. His hand was phosphorescent from skinning the fish and he watched the flow of the water against it. The flow was less strong and as he rubbed the side of his hand against the planking of the skiff, particles of phosphorus floated off and drifted slowly astern.

---

* **a leprous grey-white** : 「문둥이처럼 새파란」.
* **back** : 앞에 Being을 보충할 것.

"He is tiring or he is resting," the old man said. "Now let me get through* the eating of this dolphin and get some rest and a little sleep."

Under the stars and with the night colder all the time he ate half of one of the dolphin fillets and one of the flying fish, gutted and with its head cut off.*

"What an excellent fish dolphin is to eat cooked,*" he said. "And what a miserable fish raw.* I will never go in a boat again without salt or limes."

If I had brains I would have splashed water on the bow all day and drying,* it would have made salt, he thought. But then I did not hook the dolphin until almost sunset. Still it was a lack of preparation. But I have chewed it all well and I am not nauseated.

The sky was clouding over to the east and one after another the stars he knew were gone. It looked now as though he were moving into a great canyon of clouds and the wind had dropped.

"There will be bad weather in three or four days," he said. "But not tonight and not tomorrow. Rig now to get some sleep, old man, while the fish is calm and steady."

---

* **get through** : finish.
* **gutted and with its head cut off** : 「내장을 꺼내버린 다음 대가리도 잘라버리고서」. ate의 補語.
* **to eat cooked** : 「요리해서 먹는다면」.
* **What a miserable fish raw.** : what a miserable fish dolphin is to eat raw.
* **drying** : if it dried.

He held the line tight in his right hand and then pushed his thigh against his right hand as he leaned all his weight against the wood of the bow. Then he passed the line a little lower on his shoulders and braced his left hand on it.

My right hand can hold it* as long as it is braced,* he thought. If it relaxes in sleep my left hand will wake me as the line goes out. It is hard on the right hand. But he is used to punishment. Even if I sleep twenty minutes or a half an hour it is good. He lay forward cramping himself against the line with all of his body, putting all his weight onto his right hand, and he was asleep.

He did not dream of the lions but instead of a vast school of porpoises that stretched for eight or ten miles and it was in the time of their mating* and they would leap high into the air and return into the same hole they had made in the water when they leaped.

Then he dreamed that he was in the village on his bed and there was a norther* and he was very cold and his right arm was asleep* because his head had rested on it instead of a pillow.

After that he began to dream of the long yellow

---

* **can hold it** : 「줄을 절대로 놓지 않을 것이다」.
* **as long as it is braced** : 「줄이 팽팽한 동안은」.
* **the time of their mating** : 「고기들의 交尾期」.
* **norther** : 「寒冷北風」.
* **his right arm was asleep**에서, asleep : numb.

beach and he saw the first of the lions come down onto it in the early dark and then the other lions came and he rested his chin on the wood of the bows where the ship lay anchored with the evening off-shore breeze* and he waited to see if there would be more lions and he was happy.

The moon had been up for a long time but he slept on and the fish pulled on steadily and the boat moved into the tunnel of clouds.

He woke with the jerk of his right fist coming up against his face and the line burning out through his right hand. He had no feeling of his left hand but he braked all he could with his right and the line rushed out. Finally his left hand found the line and he leaned back against the line and now it burned his back and his left hand, and his left hand was taking all the strain and cutting badly. He looked back at the coils of line and they were feeding* smoothly. Just then the fish jumped making a great bursting of the ocean and then a heavy fall. Then he jumped again and again and the boat was going fast although line was still racing out and the old man was raising the strain to breaking point and raising it to breaking point again and again. He had been pulled down tight onto the bow and his

---

* **evening off-shore breeze** : 저녁 무렵 海岸에서 바다 쪽으로 부는 微風.
* **feeding** : going out.

face was in the cut slice of dolphin and he could not move.

This is what we waited for, he thought. So now let us take it.

Make him pay for the line,* he thought. Make him pay for it.

He could not see the fish's jumps but only heard the breaking of the ocean and the heavy splash as he fell. The speed of the line was cutting his hands badly but he had always known this would happen and he tried to keep the cutting across the calloused parts and not let the line slip into the palm nor cut the fingers.

If the boy was here he would wet the coils of line, he thought. Yes. If the boy were here. If the boy were here.

The line went out and out and out but it was slowing now and he was making the fish earn each inch of it.* Now he got his head up from the wood and out of the slice of fish that his cheek had crushed. Then he was on his knees and then he rose slowly to his feet. He was ceding line but more slowly all he time. He worked back to where he could feel with his foot the coils of line that he could not see. There was plenty of line still and now the fish had to pull the ftiction of all

* make him pay for the line : 「줄값을 물려야겠다」.

* He was making the fish earn each inch of it.: 「고기가 낚시줄을 조금씩만 끌어당기도록 조종하고 있었다」.

that new line through the water.

Yes, he thought. And now he has jumped more than a dozen times and filled the sacks along his back with air and he cannot go down deep to die where I cannot bring him up. He will start circling soon and then I must work on him. I wonder what started him so suddenly? Could it have been hunger* that made him desperate, or was he frightened by something in the night? Maybe he suddenly felt fear. But he was such a calm, strong fish and he seemed so fearless and so confident. It is strange.

"You better be fearless and confident yourself, old man," he said. "You're holding him again but you cannot get line. But soon he has to circle."

The old man held him with his left hand and his shoulders now and stooped down and scooped up water in his right hand to get the crushed dolphin flesh off of his face. He was afraid that it might nauseate him and he would vomit and lose his strength. When his face was cleaned he washed his right hand in the water over the side and then let it stay in the salt water while he watched the first light come before the sunrise. He's headed almost east, he thought. That means he is tired and going with the current. Soon he will have to circle. Then our true work begins.

* **could it have been hunger?** : could it have been for hunger?

After he judged that his right hand had been in the water long enough he took it out and looked at it.

"It is not bad," he said. "And pain does not matter to a man.*"

He took hold of the line carefully so that it did not fit into any of the fresh line cuts and shifted his weight so that he could put his left hand into the sea on the other side of the skiff.

"You did not do so badly* for something worthless," he said to his left hand. "But there was a moment when I could not find you.*"

Why was I not born with two good hands? he thought. Perhaps it was my fault in not training that one properly. But God knows he has had enough chances to learn. He did not do so badly in the night, though, and he has only cramped once. If he cramps again let the line cut him off.

When he thought that he knew that he was not being clear-headed and he thought he should chew some more of the dolphin. But I can't, he told himself. It is better to be light-headed than to lose your strength from nausea. And I know I cannot keep* it if I eat it

---

* **Pain does not matter to a man.** : 주인공(즉 작가)의 人生觀을 나타내는 문장이다. Hemingway 文学의 최고봉은 stoicism인데 이 문장은 그것을 표백한 글이다. 좀더 자세한 解說을 위해선 拙著〈研究〉pp. 261-268을 보라.
* **You did not do so badly.** :「잘 싸웠다, 잘 해냈다」.
* **I could not find you.** :「너를 몰라 보았다」.
* **keep** :「소화시키다, 새기다」.

since my face was in it. I will keep it for an emergency until it goes bad. But it is too late to try for strength* now through nourishment.* You're stupid, he told himself. Eat the other flying fish.

It was there, cleaned and ready, and he picked it up with his left hand and ate it chewing the bones carefully and eating all of it down to the tail.

It has more nourishment than almost any fish, he thought. At least the kind of strength that I need. Now I have done what I can, he thought. Let him begin to circle and let the fight come.

The sun was rising for the third time since he had put to sea* when the fish started to circle.

He could not see by the slant of the line that the fish was circling. It was too early for that. He just felt a faint slackening of the pressure of the line and be commenced to pull on* it gently with his right hand. It tightened, as always, but just when he reached the point where it would break, line began to come in.* He slipped his shoulders and head from under the line and began to pull in line steadily and gently. He used both of his hands in a swinging motion and tried to do the pulling as much as he could with his body and his legs.

- **to try for strength** : 「힘을 얻기에는」.
- **through nourishment** : 「영양을 취하여」.
- **He had put to sea.** : 「바다에 나왔다」.
- **put on** : 「당기다」.
- **began to come in** : began to slacken.

His old legs and shoulders pivoted with the swinging of the pulling.*

"It is a very big circle," he said. "But he is circling."

Then the line would not come in any more and he held it until he saw the drops jumping from it in the sun. Then it started out and the old man knelt down and let it go grudgingly back into the dark water.

"He is making* the far part of his circle now," he said. I must hold all I can, he thought. The strain will shorten his circle each time. Perhaps in an hour I will see him. Now I must convince him and then I must kill him.

But the fish kept on circling slowly and the old man was wet with sweat and tired deep into his bones two hours later. But the circles were much shorter now and from the way the line slanted he could tell the fish had risen steadily while he swam.

For an hour the old man had been seeing black spots before his eyes and the sweat salted his eyes and salted the cut over his eye and on his forehead. He was not afraid of the black spots. They were normal at the tension that he was pulling on the line. Twice, though, he had felt faint and dizzy and that had worried him.

"I could not fail myself and die on a fish like this,"

---

* **pivoted with the swinging of the pulling** : 「줄을 끌어당기는 동작의 枢軸이 되어 움직였다」.
* **is making** : is circling.

he said. "Now that I have him coming so beautifully,* God help me endure. I'll say a hundred Our Fathers and a hundred Hail Marys. But I cannot say them now."

Consider them said, he thought. I'll say them later.

Just then he felt a sudden banging and jerking on the line he held with his two hands. It was sharp and hard-feeling and heavy.

He is hitting the wire leader with his spear,* he thought. That was bound to come.* He had to do that. It may make him jump though and I would rather he stayed circling now.* The jumps were necessary for him to take air. But after that each one* can widen the opening of the hook wound and he can throw the hook.

"Don't jump, fish," he said. "Don't jump."

The fish hit the wire several times more and each time he shook his head the old man gave up a little line.

I must hold his pain where it is, he thought. Mine does not matter. I can control mine. But his pain could drive him mad.

---

* **now that I have him coming so beautifully** : 「이젠 저렇게 얌전하게 끌려오니」 *cf.* have (has) + object + present participle (or p. p.).
* **spear** : 「창같이 뾰족한 고기의 부리」.
* **That was bound to come.** : 「반드시 오고야 말 일이었다」.
* **I would rather he stayed circling now.** : I would rather wish that he stayed circling now. 「아직은 좀 더 그대로 회전이나 계속해주었으면 좋겠다」. stay : last out 「持續하다」.
* **each one** : each jump.

After a while the fish stopped beating at the wire and started circling slowly again. The old man was gaining line steadily now. But he felt faint again. He lifted some sea water with his left hand and put it on his head. Then he put more on and rubbed the back of his neck.

"I have no cramps," he said. "He'll be up soon and I can last. You have to last.·Don't even speak of it."

He kneeled against the bow and, for a moment, slipped the line over his back again. I'll rest now while he goes out on the circle and then stand up and work on him when he comes in, he decided.

It was a great temptation to rest in the bow and let the fish make one circle by himself without recovering any line. But when the strain showed the fish had turned to come toward the boat, the old man rose to his feet and started the pivoting and the weaving pulling* that brought in all the line he gained.

I'm tireder than I have ever been, he thought, and now the trade wind is rising. But that will be good to take him in with. I need that badly.

"I'll rest on the next turn as he goes out," he said. "I feel much better. Then in two or three turns more I will have him."

---

* **weaving pulling** :「전후좌우로 움직이면서 끌어당기는 것」.

His straw hat was far on the back of his head and he sank down into the bow with the pull of the line* as he felt the fish turn.

You work now, fish,* he thought. I'll take you at the turn.

The sea had risen considerably. But it was a fair-weather breeze and he had to have it to get home.

"I'll just steer south and west," he said. "A man is never lost at sea and it* is a long island."

It was on the third turn that he saw the fish first.

He saw him first as a dark shadow that took so long to pass under the boat that he could not believe its length.

"No," he said. "He can't be that big.*"

But he was that big and at the end of this circle he came to the surface only thirty yards away and the man saw his tail out of water. It was higher than a big scythe blade and a very pale lavender above the dark blue water. It raked back* and as the fish swam just below the surface the old man could see his huge bulk and the purple stripes that banded him. His dorsal fin was down and his huge pectorals were spread wide.

---

* **He sank down ... of the line.** : 「이물에 주저앉아 줄을 끌어당겼다.」
* **You work now, fish.** : 「잘도 온다, 고기야」. work = move, come in.
* **it** : Cuba.
* **that big** : big like that. that는 副詞.
* **raked back** : 「뒤로 기울었다」.

On this circle the old man could see the fish's eye and the two gray sucking fish that swam around him. Sometimes they attached themselves to him. Sometimes they darted off. Sometimes they would swim easily in his shadow. They were each over three feet long and when they swam fast they lashed their whole bodies like eels.

The old man was sweating now but from something else besides the sun. On each calm placid turn the fish made he was gaining line and he was sure that in two turns more he would have a chance to get the harpoon in.

But I must get him close, close, close, he thought. I mustn't try for the head. I must get the heart.

"Be calm and strong, old man," he said.

On the next circle the fish's back was out but he was a little too far from the boat. On the next circle he was still too far away but he was higher out of water and the old man was sure that by gaining some more line he could have him alongside.

He had rigged his harpoon long before and its coil of light rope was in a round basket and the end was made fast to the bitt in the bow.

The fish was coming in on his circle* now calm and beautiful looking and only his great tail moving. The

---

* **coming in on his circle** : 「빙빙 돌며 들어온다」.

old man pulled on* him all* that he could to bring him closer. For just a moment the fish turned a little on his side. Then he straightened himself and began another circle.

"I moved him," the old man said. "I moved him then."

He felt faint again now but he held on* the great fish all the strain that he could. I moved him, he thought. Maybe this time I can get him over. Pull, hands, he thought. Hold up, legs. Last for me, head. Last for me. You never went. This time I'll pull him over.

But when he put all of his effort on, starting it well out before the fish came alongside and pulling with all his strength, the fish pulled part way over* and then righted himself and swam away.

"Fish," the old man said. "Fish, you are going to have to die anyway. Do you have to kill me too?"

That way nothing is accomplished,* he thought. His mouth was too dry to speak but he could not reach for the water now. I must get him alongside this time, he thought. I am not good for many more turns.* Yes you

---

* **pulled on** : 「끌어당겼다」.
* **all** : 「전력을 다하여」
* **held on** : clung to.
* **pulled part way over** : rolled over a little.
* **That way nothing is accomplished.** : Nothing is accomplished that way. that way : if you kill me also.
* **I am not good for many more turns.** : 「이 이상 더 돌리다가는 되려 못견디겠다」. good : strong enough.

are,* he told himself. You're good for ever.

On the next turn, he nearly had him. But again the fish righted himself and swam slowly away.

You are killing me, fish, the old man thought. But you have a right to. Never have I seen a greater, or more beautiful, or a calmer or more noble thing than you, brother. Come on and kill me. I do not care who kills who.*

Now you are getting confused in the head, he thought. You must keep your head clear. Keep your head clear and know how to suffer like a man. Or a fish,* he thought.

"Clear up, head," he said in a voice he could hardly hear. "Clear up."

Twice more it was the same on the turns.*

I do not know, the old man thought. He had been on the point of feeling himself go* each time. I do not know. But I will try it once more.

He tried it once more and he felt himself going* when he turned the fish. The fish righted himself and swam off again slowly with the great tail weaving in

---

* **Yes, you are.** : Yes, you are good.
* **I do not care who kills who.** : ~ who kills whom이 올바른 語法이나, 이렇게 쓰인 것은 who와 whom을 혼동할 만큼 동요된 상태를 나타낸다.
* **or a fish** : or know how to suffer like a fish.
* **Twice more … on the turns.** : It was all the same though the fish turned twice more.
* **go, going** : faint, fainting.

the air.

I'll try it again, the old man promised, although his hands were mushy now and he could only see well in flashes.*

He tried it again and it was the same. So he thought, and he felt himself going* before he started; I will try it once again.

He took all his pain and what was left of his strength and his long gone pride and he put it* against the fish's agony and the fish came over onto his side and swam gently on his side, his bill almost touching the planking of the skiff and started to pass the boat, long, deep, wide, silver and barred* with purple and interminable* in the water.

The old man dropped the line and put his foot on it and lifted the harpoon as high as he could and drove it down with all his strength, and more strength he had just summoned, into the fish's side just behind the great chest fin that rose high in the air to the altitude of the man's chest. He felt the iron go in and he leaned on it and drove it further and then pushed all his weight after it.

Then the fish came alive, with his death in him,* and

---

* **in flashes** : 「눈도 까불거리며, 순간적으로」.
* **it** : all his pain, what was left of his strength, and his long gone pride를 총괄한 代名詞.
* **barred** : marked with stripes. 「자색 줄무늬로 아롱진」. pass의 補語.
* **interminable** : 「끝없이 크게 보이며」. pass의 補語.
* **with his death in him** : 「몸에 致命傷을 입고서」.

rose high out of the water showing all his great length and width and all his power and his beauty. He seemed to hang in the air above the old man in the skiff. Then he fell into the water with a crash that sent spray over the old man and over all of the skiff.

The old man felt faint and sick and he could not see well. But he cleared the harpoon line and let it run slowly through his raw hands* and, when he could see, he saw the fish was on his back with his silver belly up. The shaft of the harpoon was projecting at an angle* from the fish's shoulder and the sea was discolouring with the red of the blood from his heart. First it was dark as a shoal in the blue water that was more than a mile deep. Then it spread like a cloud. The fish was silvery and still and floated with the waves.

The old man looked carefully in the glimpse of vision* that he had. Then he took two turns of the harpoon line around the bitt in the bow and laid his head on his hands.

"Keep my head clear," he said against the wood of the bow. "I am a tired old man. But I have killed this fish which is my brother and now I must do the slave work*."

Now I must prepare the nooses and the rope to lash

---

* **raw hands** :「껍질이 벗겨져서 쓰라린 손」.
* **at an angle** :「똑바로」.
* **the glimpse of vision** :「흘끗 눈에 보인 듯한 幻像」.
* **slave work** :「고된 雜役」.

him alongside, he thought. Even if we were two and swamped her to load him and bailed her out,* this skiff would never hold him. I must prepare everything, then bring him in and lash him well and step the mast* and set sail for home.

He started to pull the fish in to have him alongside so that he could pass a line through his gills and out his mouth and make his head fast alongside the bow. I want to see him, he thought, and to touch and to feel him. He is my fortune, he thought. But that is not why I wish to feel him. I think I felt his heart, he thought. When I pushed on the harpoon shaft the second time. Bring him in now and make him fast and get the noose around his tail and another around his middle to bind him to the skiff.

"Get to work, old man," he said. He took a very small drink of the water. "There is very much slave work to be done now that the fight is over."

He looked up at the sky and then out to his fish. He looked at the sun carefully. It is not much more than noon, he thought. And the trade wind is rising. The lines all mean nothing now. The boy and I will splice them when we are home.

"Come on, fish," he said. But the fish did not come.

---

* **Even if we were ... bailed her out.** :「비록 배에 탈 사람은 우리 둘(나와 고기) 밖에 없지만 이 놈을 실어서 배에 물이 고이면 아무리 물을 퍼낸다 하더라도」. swamp : 浸水시키다.
* **step the mast** :「돛을 달다」.

Instead he lay there wallowing now in the seas and the old man pulled the skiff up-onto him.

When he was even with him* and had the fish's head against the bow* he could not believe his size. But he untied the harpoon rope from the bitt, passed it through the fish's gills and out his jaws, made a turn around his sword* then passed the rope through the other gill, made another turn around the bill and knotted the double rope and made it fast to the bitt in the bow. He cut the rope then and went astern to noose the tail. The fish had turned silver from his original purple and silver, and the stripes showed the same pale violet colour as his tail. They were wider than a man's hand with his fingers spread and the fish's eye looked as detached* as the mirrors in a periscope or as a saint in a procession.

"It was the only way to kill him," the old man said. He was feeling better since the water* and he knew he would not go away* and his head was clear. He's over fifteen hundred pounds the way he is,* he thought.

- **He was even with him.** : 「고기와 나란히 섰다」.
- **have the fish's head against the bow** : 「고기의 머리를 이물에 잡아 매다」. have : tie.
- **made a turn around his sword** : 「뾰족한 주둥이에 한바퀴 감았다」.
- **looked detached** : 「초연하게 보였다. 초탈한 표정이었다」.
- **mirrors in a periscope** : 「潜望鏡의 반사경」.
- **since the water** : after drinking water.
- **go away** : faint.
- **the way he is** : 「현재로는」.

Maybe much more. If he dresses out two-thirds of that at thirty cents a pound?*

"I need a pencil for that," he said. "My head is not that clear. But I think the great DiMaggio would be proud of me today. I had no bone spurs. But the hands and the back hurt truly." I wonder what a bone spur is, he thought. Maybe we have them without knowing of it.

He made the fish fast to bow and stern and to the middle thwart. He was so big it was like lashing a much bigger skiff alongside. He cut a piece of line and tied the fish's lower jaw against his bill so his mouth would not open and they would sail as cleanly as possible. Then he stepped the mast and, with the stick that was his gaff and with his boom rigged, the patched sail drew,* the boat began to move, and half lying in the stern he sailed south-west.

He did not need a compass to tell him where south-west was. He only needed the feel* of the trade wind and the drawing of the sail. I better put a small line out with a spoon on it and try and get something to eat and drink for the moisture.* But he could not find a

---

* **If he dresses out ... a pound?** :「내장 같은 것을 죄다 손질해 버리고 3분의 2만 고기로 만들어서 한 파운드에 30센트씩 받는다면?」.
* **with the stick ... the patched sail drew** :「縱帆 상부에 斜桁으로 쓰였던 막대기와 아랫도리 활죽으로 장비를 갖추고, 아울러 더덕더덕 기운 돛을 달고서」.
* **the feel** :「風勢」.
* **for the moisture** :「목을 추기려고」.

spoon and his sardines were rotten. So he hooked a patch of yellow Gulf weed with the gaff as they passed and shook it so that the small shrimps that were in it fell onto the planking of the skiff. There were more than a dozen of them and they jumped and kicked like sand fleas. The old man pinched their heads off with his thumb and forefinger and ate them chewing up the shells and the tails. They were very tiny but he knew they were nourishing and they tasted good.

The old man still had two drinks of water in the bottle and he used half of one after he had eaten the shrimps. The skiff was sailing well considering the handicaps* and he steered with the tiller under his arm. He could see the fish and he had only to look at his hands and feel his back against the stern to know that this had truly happened and was not a dream. At one time when he was feeling so badly toward the end,* he had thought perhaps it was a dream. Then when he had seen the fish come out of the water and hang motionless in the sky before he fell, he was sure there was some great strangeness and he could not believe it. Then he could not see well, although now he saw as well as ever.

Now he knew there was the fish and his hands and

---

* **considering the handicaps** : 「배 옆에 큰 짐을 달고 있다는 어려움을 생각할 때」.
* **toward the end** : 「고기와의 결투가 끝날 무렵」.

back were no dream. The hands cure quickly, he thought. I bled them clean* and the salt water will heal them. The dark water of the true gulf is the greatest healer that there is. All I must do is keep the head clear.* The hands have done their work and we sail well. With his mouth shut and his tail straight up and down we sail like brothers. Then his head started to become a little unclear and he thought, is he bringing me in or am I bringing him in? If I were towing him behind there would be no question. Nor if the fish were in the skiff, with all dignity gone,* there would be no question either. But they were sailing together lashed side by side and the old man thought, let him bring me in if it pleases him. I am only better than him through trickery* and he meant me no harm.

They sailed well and the old man soaked his hands in the salt water and tried to keep his head clear. There were high cumulus clouds and enough cirrus above them so that the old man knew the breeze would last all night. The old man looked at the fish constantly to make sure it was true. It was an hour before the first shark hit him.

The shark was not an accident. He had come up

---

* **bled them clean** :「손에서 피가 나올대로 나왔다」.
* **All I must do is keep the head clear.** : keep 앞에 to를 보충해 볼 것. 口語体에서는 to를 생략하는 것이 통례이다.
* **with all dignity gone** :「모든 위엄을 잃은 채」.
* **through trickery** :「계교에 있어서는」.

from deep down in the water as the dark cloud of blood had settled and dispersed in the mile deep sea. He had come up so fast and absolutely without caution that he broke the surface of the blue water and was in the sun. Then he fell back into the sea and picked up the scent and started swimming on the course the skiff and the fish had taken.

Sometimes he lost the scent. But he would pick it up again, or have just a trace of it, and he swam fast and hard on the course. He was a very big Mako shark* built to swim as fast as the fastest fish in the sea and everything about him was beautiful except his jaws. His back was as blue as a sword fish's* and his belly was silver and his hide was smooth and handsome. He was built as a sword fish except for his huge jaws which were tight shut now as he swam fast, just under the surface with his high dorsal fin knifing through the water without wavering. Inside the closed double lip of his jaws all of his eight rows of teeth were slanted inwards. They were not the ordinary pyramid-shaped teeth of most sharks. They were shaped like a man's fingers when they are crisped like claws. They were nearly as long as the fingers of the old man and they had razor-sharp cutting edges on both sides. This was a fish built to feed on all the fishes in the sea, that were

* **Mako shark** : 「주둥이가 뾰죽한 상어」.
* **swordfish** : 「황새치」.

so fast and strong and well armed that they had no other enemy. Now he speeded up as he smelled the fresher scent and his blue dorsal fin cut the water.

When the old man saw him coming he knew that this was a shark that had no fear at all and would do exactly what he wished. He prepared the harpoon and made the rope fast while he watched the shark come on. The rope was short as it lacked* what he had cut away to lash the fish.

The old man's head was clear and good now and he was full of resolution but he had little hope. It was too good to last, he thought. He took one look at the great fish as he watched the shark close in. It might as well* have been a dream, he thought. I cannot keep him from hitting me but maybe I can get him. *Dentuso*,* he thought. Bad luck to your mother.*

The shark closed fast astern and when he hit the fish the old man saw his mouth open and his strange eyes and the clicking chop of the teeth as he drove forward in the meat just above the tail. The shark's head was out of water and his back was coming out and the old man could hear the noise of skin and flesh ripping on the big fish when he rammed the harpoon down onto the shark's head at a spot where the line between

---

* **as it lacked** :「(베어버린 부분이) 없어졌기 때문에」
* **might as well ～** :「～라면 좋았을 걸」.
* ***Dentuso*** [dentu:so] : (Sp.) 이빨이 크고 고르지 않은 상어의 일종.
* **Bad luck to your mother.** :「망할 놈의 자식 같으니」.

his eyes intersected with the line that ran straight back from his nose. There were no such lines. There was only the heavy sharp blue head and the big eyes and the clicking, thrusting all-swallowing jaws. But that was the location of the brain and the old man hit it. He hit it with his blood mushed hands driving a good harpoon with all his strength. He hit it without hope but with resolution and complete malignancy.

The shark swung over and the old man saw his eye was not alive and then he swung over once again, wrapping himself in two loops of the rope. The old man knew that he was dead but the shark would not accept it. Then, on his back,* with his tail lashing and his jaws clicking, the shark plowed over the water as a speedboat does. The water was white where his tail beat it and three-quarters of his body was clear above the water when the rope came taut, shivered, and then snapped.* The shark lay quietly for a little while on the surface and the old man watched him. Then he went down very slowly.

"He took about forty pounds," the old man said aloud. He took my harpoon too and all the rope, he thought, and now my fish bleeds again and there will be others.

He did not like to look at the fish anymore since he

* **on his back** : 「나자빠진 채」.
* **snapped** : broke suddenly.

had been mutilated. When the fish had been hit it was as though he himself were hit.

But I killed the shark that hit my fish, he thought. And he was the biggest *dentuso* that I have ever seen. And God knows that I have seen big ones.

It was too good to last, he thought. I wish it had been a dream now and that I had never hooked the fish and was alone in bed on the newspapers.

"But man is not made for defeat,*" he said. "A man can be destroyed but not defeated."* I am sorry that I killed the fish though, he thought. Now the bad time is coming and I do not even have the harpoon. The *dentuso* is cruel and able and strong and intelligent. But I was more intelligent than he was. Perhaps not, he thought. Perhaps I was only better armed.

"Don't think, old man," he said aloud. "Sail on this course and take it when it comes*."

But I must think, he thought. Because it is all I have left. That and baseball. I wonder how the great DiMaggio would have liked the way* I hit him in the brain? It was no great thing, he thought. Any man could do it. But do you think my hands were as great a

* **Man is not made for defeat. A man can be destroyed but not defeated.** : 이 문장도 p. 의 문장 'Pain does not matter to a man'.과 아울러 Hemingway의 人生觀 내지 倫理觀을 첨예하게 나타낸 문장이다. 拙著 〈硏究〉 pp.261-268을 참조.
* **take it when it comes** : 「상어놈이 오거든 맞서봐」.
* **the way** : 「솜씨」.

handicap as the bone spurs? I cannot know. I never had anything wrong with my heel except the time the sting ray* stung it when I stepped on him when swimming and paralyzed the lower leg and made the unbearable pain.

"Think about something cheerful, old man," he said. "Every minute now you are closer to home. You sail lighter for the loss of forty pounds."

He knew quite well the pattern of what could happen when he reached the inner part of the current. But there was nothing to be done now.

"Yes there is," he said aloud. "I can lash my knife to the butt of one of the oars."

So he did that with the tiller under his arm and the sheet of the sail under his foot.

"Now," he said. "I am still an old man. But I am not unarmed."

The breeze was fresh now and he sailed on well. He watched only the forward part of the fish and some of his hope returned.

It is silly not to hope, he thought. Besides I believe it is a sin. Do not think about sin, he thought. There are enough problems now without sin.* Also I have no understanding of it.

I have no understanding of it and I am not sure that

---

* **sting ray** : 가오리의 일종.
* **without sin** : besides sin.

I believe in it. Perhaps it was a sin to kill the fish. I suppose it was* even though I did it to keep me alive and feed many people. But then everything is a sin. Do not think about sin. It is much too late for that and there are people who are paid to do it.* Let them think about it. You were born to be a fisherman as the fish was born to be a fish. San Pedro* was a fisherman as was the father of the great DiMaggio.*

But he liked to think about all things that he was involved in and since there was nothing to read and he did not have a radio, he thought much and he kept on thinking about sin. You did not kill the fish only to keep alive and to sell for food, he thought. You killed him for pride and because you are a fisherman. You loved him when he was alive and you loved him after. If you love him, it is not a sin to kill him. Or is it more?

"You think too much, old man," he said aloud.

But you enjoyed killing the *dentuso*, he thought. He lives on the live fish as you do. He is not a scavenger nor just a moving appetite* as some sharks are. He is beautiful and noble and knows no fear of anything.

---

* **it was** : it was a sin to kill the fish.
* **who are paid to do it** : 「돈을 받고 그런 문제를 생각하는」.do : think.
* ***San Pedro*** [san pédro] : Saint Peter의 스페인名. Galilee海의 어부로 있다가 예수의 12사도 중의 한 사람이 되었다.
* **as was the father of the great DiMaggio** : as the father of the great DiMaggio was fisherman.
* **a moving appetite** : 「대단한 식욕을 가진 놈」.

"I killed him in self-defense," the old man said aloud. "And I killed him well."

Besides, he thought, everything kills everything else in some way. Fishing kills me exactly as it keeps me alive. The boy keeps me alive, he thought. I must not deceive myself too much.

He leaned over the side and pulled loose* a piece of the meat of the fish where the shark had cut him. He chewed it and noted its quality and its good taste. It was firm and juicy, like meat, but it was not red. There was no stringiness in it and he knew that it would bring the highest price in the market. But there was no way to keep its scent out of the water and the old man knew that a very bad time was coming.

The breeze was steady. It had backed a little further into the north-east and he knew that meant that it would not fall off.* The old man looked ahead of him but he could see no sails nor could he see the hull nor the smoke of any ship. There were only the flying fish that went up from his bow sailing away to either side and the yellow patches of Gulf weed. He could not even see a bird.

He had sailed for two hours, resting in the stern and sometimes chewing a bit of the meat from the marlin, trying to rest and to be strong, when he saw the first of

* pulled loose : 「떼었다」.
* fall off : 「약해지다」.

the two sharks.

"Ay," he said aloud. There is no translation for this word and perhaps it is just a noise such as a man might make, involuntarily, feeling the nail go through his hands and into the wood.

"Galanos,"* he said aloud. He had seen the second fin now coming up behind the first and had identified them as shovel-nosed sharks by the brown, triangular fin and the sweeping movements of the tail. They had the scent and were excited and in the stupidity of their great hunger they were losing and finding the scent in their excitement. But they were closing all the time.

The old man made the sheet fast* and jammed the tiller.* Then he took up the oar with the knife lashed to it. He lifted it as lightly as he could because his hands rebelled at the pain. Then he opened and closed them on it* lightly to loosen them. He closed them firmly so they would take the pain now and would not flinch and watched the sharks come. He could see their wide, flattened, shovel-pointed heads now and their white-tipped wide pectoral fins. They were hateful sharks, bad smelling, scavengers as well as killers, and when they were hungry they would bite at an oar or the rudder of a boat. It was these sharks that would cut the

---

* ***Galano*** [galano] : (Sp.) 상어의 일종.
* **made the sheet fast** :「돛을 꽉 잡아 매었다」. sheet : sail.
* **jammed the tiller** :「키의 손잡이를 돌지 못하게 꼭 끼어 놓았다」.
* **them on it** :「노를 잡은 두 손」.

turtles' legs and flippers off when the turtles were asleep on the surface, and they would hit a man in the water, if they were hungry, even if the man had no smell of fish blood nor of fish slime on him.

"*Ay*," the old man said. "*Galanos*. Come on *galanos*."

They came. But they did not come as the Mako had come. One turned and went out of sight under the skiff and the old man could feel the skiff shake as he jerked and pulled on the fish. The other watched the old man with his slitted yellow eyes and then came in fast with his half circle of jaws wide to hit the fish where he had already been bitten. The line showed clearly on the top of his brown head and back where the brain joined the spinal cord* and the old man drove the knife on the oar into the juncture, withdrew it, and drove it in again into the shark's yellow cat-like eyes. The shark let go of* the fish and slid down, swallowing what he had taken as he died.

The skiff was still shaking with the destruction the other shark was doing to the fish and the old man let go the sheet so that the skiff would swing broadside and bring the shark out from under. When he saw the shark he leaned over the side and punched at him. He

---

* **spinal cord** : 「척주」.
* **let go of** : loose hold of, 「~을 놓다」.

hit only meat* and the hide was set hard* and he barely got the knife in. The blow hurt not only his hands but his shoulder too. But the shark came up fast with his head out and the old man hit him squarely in the center of his flat-topped head as his nose came out of water and lay against the fish. The old man withdrew the blade and punched the shark exactly in the same spot again. He still hung to the fish with his jaws hooked and the old man stabbed him in his left eye. The shark still hung there.

"No?" the old man said and he drove the blade between the vertebrae and the brain. It was an easy shot now and he felt the cartilage sever. The old man reversed the oar and put the blade between the shark's jaws to open them. He twisted the blade and as the shark slid loose he said, "Go on, *galano*.* Slide down a mile deep. Go see your friend, or maybe it's your mother."

The old man wiped the blade of his knife and laid down the oar. Then he found the sheet and the sail filled and he brought the skiff onto her course.

---

* **He hit only meat.** :「急所를 놓치고 말았다」는 뜻.
* **The hide was set hard.**:「가죽이 굳었다」.
* ***Galano*** : 같은 敵이면서도 Galano와 Marlin에 대한 노인의 태도를 보라. Marlin은 造物主의 攝理를 존중하고 있기 때문에 汎愛精神을 느끼나, 그것을 무시하고 있는 Galano에 대해서는 憎惡만을 느낀다. 이처럼 노인의 汎愛精神은 무한정의 것이 아니고, 자연의 攝理를 용인하는 범위 내에만 국한된 것이다. 좀 더 자세한 解說을 위해선 拙著 〈研究〉 pp.181-185를 보라.

"They must have taken a quarter of him and of the best meat," he said aloud. "I wish it were a dream and that I had never hooked him. I'm sorry about it, fish. It makes everything wrong." He stopped and he did not want to look at the fish now. Drained of blood and awash* he looked the colour of the silver backing of a mirror and his stripes still showed.

"I shouldn't have gone out so far, fish," he said. "Neither for you nor for me. I'm sorry, fish."

Now, he said to himself. Look to the lashing on the knife* and see if it has been cut. Then get your hand in order because there still is more to come.

"I wish I had a stone for the knife*," the old man said after he had checked the lashing on the oar butt. "I should have brought a stone." You should have brought many things, he thought. But you did not bring them, old man. Now is no time to think of what you do not have. Think of what you can do with what there is.

"You give me much good counsel," he said aloud. "I'm tired of it."

He held the tiller under his arm and soaked both his hands in the water as the skiff drove forward.

---

* **drained of blood and awash** : Being drained of blood and awash, 「피를 흘리고 물에 씻기어」.
* **look to the lashing on the knife** : 「칼을 비끄러맨 데를 조사하다」.
* **a stone for the knife** : 「숫돌」.

"God knows how much that last one took,*" he said. "But she's much lighter now." He did not want to think of the mutilated under-side of the fish. He knew that each of the jerking bumps of the shark had been meat torn away and that the fish now made a trail for all sharks as wide as a highway through the sea.

He was a fish to keep a man all winter,* he thought. Don't think of that. Just rest and try to get your hands in shape* to defend what is left of him. The blood smell from my hands means nothing now with* all that scent in the water. Besides they do not bleed much. There is nothing cut that means anything.* The bleeding may keep the left from cramping.*

What can I think of now? he thought. Nothing. I must think of nothing and wait for the next ones. I wish it had really been a dream, he thought. But who knows? It might have turned out well.

The next shark that came was a single shovelnose.

---

* **God knows how much that last one took.** 에서, God knows : 「아무도 모른다」. how much : how much meat. last one : last shark. took : bit away.
* **He was a fish to keep a man all winter.** : 「그만한 고기라면 겨우내 먹고 지낼 만한 것이었다」.
* **Try to get your hands in shape.** : 「손이나 제대로 쓸 수 있도록 해봐라」.
* **means nothing now with ～** : 「～에 비하면 문제가 아니다」.
* **There is nothing cut that means anything.** : 「대수롭게 여길 만한 상처는 아니다」. nothing : unimportant thing. anything : a thing of any value.
* **The bleeding may keep the left from cramping.** : 「피를 흘렸기 때문에 왼손엔 쥐가 안날지도 모른다」. the left : left hand.

He came like a pig to the trough if a pig had a mouth so wide that you could put your head in it. The old man let him hit the fish and then drove the knife on the oar down into his brain. But the shark jerked backwards as he rolled and the knife blade snapped.

The old man settled himself to steer. He did not even watch the big shark sinking slowly in the water, showing first life-size, then small, then tiny. That always fascinated the old man. But he did not even watch it now.

"I have the gaff now," he said. "But it will do no good. I have the two oars and the tiller and the short club."

Now they have beaten me, he thought. I am too old to club sharks to death. But I will try it as long as I have the oars and the short club and the tiller.

He put his hands in the water again to soak them. It was getting late in the afternoon and he saw nothing but the sea and the sky. There was more wind in the sky than there had been, and soon he hoped that he would see land.

"You're tired, old man," he said. "You're tired inside."

The sharks did not hit him again until just before sunset.

The old man saw the brown fins coming along the wide trail the fish must make in the water. They were not even quartering on the scent.* They were headed straight for the skiff swimming side by side.

He jammed the tiller, made the sheet fast and reached under the stern for the club. It was an oar handle from a broken oar sawed off to about two and a half feet in length. He could only use it effectively with one hand because of the grip of the handle* and he took good hold of it with his right hand, flexing his hand on it,* as he watched the sharks come. They were both *galanos*.

I must let the first one get a good hold* and hit him on the point of the nose or straight across the top of the head, he thought.

The two sharks closed together and as he saw the one nearest him open his jaws and sink them into the silver side of the fish, he raised the club high and brought it down heavy and slamming onto the top of the shark's broad head. He felt the rubbery solidity as the club came down. But he felt the rigidity of bone too and he struck the shark once more hard across the point of the nose as he slid down from the fish.

The other shark had been in and out and now came

---

* **quartering on the scent** : 「냄새를 따라 이리저리 찾아다녔다」.
* **grip of the handle** : 「손잡이의 잡는 데」.
* **flexing his hand on it** : 「그것을 잡은 한손을 굽혔다 폈다 하면서」.
* **Let the first one get a good hold** : 「첫번째 놈으로 하여금 마음껏 물어뜯게 하다」.

in again with his jaws wide. The old man could see pieces of the meat of the fish spilling white* from the corner of his jaws as he bumped the fish and closed his jaws. He swung at him and hit only the head and the shark looked at him and wrenched the meat loose.* The old man swung the club down on him again as he slipped away to swallow and hit only the heavy solid rubberiness.

"Come on, *galano,*" the old man said. "Come in again."

The shark came in a rush and the old man hit him as he shut his jaws. He hit him solidly and from as high up as he could raise the club. This time he felt* the bone at the base of the brain and he hit him again in the same place while the shark tore the meat loose sluggishly and slid down from the fish.

The old man watched for him to come again but neither shark showed. Then he saw one on the surface swimming in circles.* He did not see the fin of the other.

I could not expect to kill them, he thought. I could have in my time.* But I have hurt them both badly and

---

* **spilling white** : 「하얗게 흘리는」.
* **wrenched the meat loose** : 「살을 물고 비틀어 뜯었다」.
* **felt** : 「~에 맞은 것 같았다」.
* **swimming in circles** : 「빙빙 돌며 헤엄치고 있는 것을」.
* **I could have in my time.**: I could have killed them in my time. in my time : 「내 한창 때라면」.

neither one can feel very good.* If I could have used a bat with two hands I could have killed the first one surely. Even now, he thought.

He did not want to look at the fish. He knew that half of him had been destroyed. The sun had gone down while he had been in the fight with the sharks.

"It will be dark soon," he said. "Then I should see the glow of Havana. If I am too far to the eastward I will see the lights of one of the new beaches.*"

I cannot be too far out now, he thought. I hope no one has been too worried. There is only the boy to worry, of course. But I am sure he would have confidence. Many of the older fishermen will worry. Many others too, he thought. I live in a good town.

He could not talk to the fish anymore because the fish had been ruined too badly. Then something came into his head.

"Half fish,*" he said. "Fish that you were.* I am sorry that I went too far out. I ruined us both. But we have killed many sharks, you and I, and ruined many others. How many did you ever kill, old fish? You do not have that spear on your head for nothing.*"

---

* **feel very good** : 「기분이 매우 좋다」.
* **new beaches** : other beaches, unfamiliar beaches.
* **half-fish** : 「이제는 반동강이가 되고 말았구나」.
* **fish that you were** : 「그처럼 당당하더니」, 「고기라는 건 너의 지난 날의 모습이구나」.
* **for nothing** : without any purpose.

He liked to think of the fish and what he could do to a shark if he were swimming free. I should have chopped the bill off* to fight them with, he thought. But there was no hatchet and then there was no knife.

But if I had, and could have lashed it to an oar butt, what a weapon.* Then we might have fought them together. What will you do now if they come in the night? What can you do?

"Fight them," he said. "I'll fight them until I die."

But in the dark now and no glow showing and no lights and only the wind and the steady pull of the sail he felt that perhaps he was already dead. He put his two hands together and felt* the palms. They were not dead and he could bring the pain of life by simply opening and closing them. He leaned his back against the stern and knew he was not dead. His shoulders told him.

I have all those prayers I promised if I caught the fish, he thought. But I am too tired to say them now. I better get the sack and put it over my shoulders.

He lay in the stern and steered and watched for the glow to come in the sky. I have half of him, he thought. Maybe I'll have the luck to bring the forward half in.* I should have some luck. No, he said. You vio-

* **chopped the bill off** : 「주둥이를 맨 밧줄을 끊어버리고」.
* **what a weapon** : what a good weapon it would be.
* **felt** : touched.
* **forward half** : front half of the fish.

lated your luck when you went too far outside.

"Don't be silly," he said aloud. "And keep awake and steer. You may have much luck yet.

"I'd like to buy some if there's any place they sell it," he said.

What could I buy it with? he asked himself. Could I buy it with a lost harpoon and a broken knife and two bad hands?

"You might," he said. "You tried to buy it with eighty-four days at sea. They nearly sold it to you too."

I must not think nonsense, he thought. Luck is a thing that comes in many forms and who can recognize her? I would take some though in any form and pay what they asked. I wish I could see the glow from the lights, he thought. I wish too many things. But that is the thing I wish for now. He tried to settle more comfortably to steer and from his pain he knew he was not dead.

He saw the reflected glare of the lights of the city at what must have been around ten o'clock at night.* They were only perceptible at first as the light is in the sky before the moon rises. Then they were steady to see across the ocean which was rough now with the increasing breeze. He steered inside of the glow and he thought that now, soon, he must hit* the edge of the

* **at what must ... at night** : 「밤 10시가 되었으리라 생각될 무렵」.
* **hit** : arrive at. 「부딪치다, 당도하다」.

stream.

Now it is over, he thought. They will probably hit me again. But what can a man do against them in the dark without a weapon?

He was stiff and sore now and his wounds and all of the strained parts of his body hurt with the cold of the night. I hope I do not have to fight again, he thought. I hope so much I do not have to fight again.

But by midnight he fought and this time he knew the fight was useless. They came in a pack* and he could only see the lines in the water that their fins made and their phosphorescence as they threw themselves on the fish. He clubbed at heads and heard the jaws chop and the shaking of the skiff as they took hold below.* He clubbed desperately at what he could only feel and hear and he felt something seize the club and it was gone.

He jerked the tiller free from the rudder and beat and chopped with it, holding it in both hands and driving it down again and again. But they were up to the bow now and driving in one after the other and together, tearing off the pieces of meat that showed glowing below the sea as they turned to come once more.

One came, finally, against the head itself and he knew that it was over. He swung the tiller across the

* **came in a pack** : 「떼를 지어 몰려왔다」.
* **took hold below** : 「배 밑에서 물고 늘어졌다」.

shark's head where the jaws were caught in the heaviness of the fish's head* which would not tear. He swung it once and twice and again. He heard the tiller break and he lunged at the shark with the splintered butt. He felt it go in and knowing it was sharp he drove it in again. The shark let go and rolled away. That was the last shark of the pack that came. There was nothing more for them to eat.

The old man could hardly breathe now and he felt a strange taste in his mouth. It was coppery and sweet and he was afraid of it for a moment. But there was not much of it.

He spat into the ocean and said, "Eat that, *galanos*. And make a dream you've killed a man."

He knew he was beaten now finally and without remedy and he went back to the stern and found the jagged end of the tiller would fit in the slot of the rudder well enough for him to steer. He settled the sack around his shoulders and put the skiff on her course. He sailed lightly now and he had no thoughts nor any feelings of any kind. He was past everything now and he sailed the skiff to make his home port as well and as intelligently as he could. In the night sharks hit the carcass as someone might pick up crumbs from the table. The old man paid no attention

---

* where the jaws … the fish's head : 「고기의 딱딱한 머리를 물고 있는」.

to them and did not pay any attention to anything except steering. He only noticed how lightly and how well the skiff sailed now* there was no great weight beside her.

She's good, he thought. She is sound and not harmed in any way except for the tiller. That is easily replaced.

He could feel he was inside the current now and he could see the lights of the beach colonies along the shore. He knew where he was now and it was nothing to get home.

The wind is our friend,* anyway, he thought. Then he added, sometimes. And the great sea with our friends and our enemies. And bed, he thought. Bed is my friend.* Just bed, he thought. Bed will be a great thing. It is easy when you are beaten, he thought. I never knew how easy it was. And what beat you, he thought.

"Nothing," he said aloud. "I went out too far."

When he sailed into the little harbour the lights of the Terrace were out and he knew everyone was in bed. The breeze had risen steadily and was blowing strongly now. It was quiet in the harbour though and he sailed up onto the little patch of shingle below the

---

* **now** : now that; since.
* **The wind is our friend. Bed is my friend** : 작가의 汎愛精神을 극명하게 보여주는 문장들이다.

rocks. There was no one to help him so he pulled the boat up as far as he could. Then he stepped out and made her fast to a rock.

He unstepped the mast and furled the sail and tied it. Then he shouldered the mast and started to climb. It was then he knew the depth of his tiredness. He stopped for a moment and looked back and saw in the reflection from the street light the great tail of the fish standing up well behind the skiff's stern. He saw the white naked line of his backbone and the dark mass of the head with the projecting bill and all the nakedness between.

He started to climb again and at the top he fell and lay for some time with the mast across his shoulder.* He tried to get up. But it was too difficult and he sat there with the mast on his shoulder and looked at the road. A cat passed on the far side going about its business and the old man watched it. Then he just watched the road.

Finally he put the mast down and stood up. He picked the mast up and put it on his shoulder and started up the road. He had to sit down five times* before he reached his shack.

---

* **He fell ... across his shoulder.**: 예수가 十字架를 지고서 쓰러진 모습의 imagery를 느끼게 한다. 이에 대한 자세한 解說을 위해선 拙著 〈研究〉 pp.228-231을 보라.
* **He had to sit down five times.**: Santiago가 다섯번 주저앉았음에 비해, 예수는 세번 주저앉았다. numerology of Christianity의 導用이다.

Inside the shack he leaned the mast against the wall. In the dark he found a water bottle and took a drink. Then he lay down on the bed. He pulled the blanket over his shoulders and then over his back and legs and he slept face down on the newspapers with his arms out straight and the palms of his hands up.*

He was asleep when the boy looked in the door in the morning. It was blowing so hard that the drifting-boats would not be going out and the boy had slept late and then come to the old man's shack as he had come each morning. The boy saw that the old man was breathing and then he saw the old man's hands and he started to cry. He went out very quietly to go to bring some coffee and all the way down the road he was crying.*

Many fishermen were around the skiff looking at what was lashed beside it and one was in the water, his trousers rolled up, measuring the skeleton with a length of line.

---

* **He slept face down ... his hands up.** : 이 imagery는 예수가 十字架에 매달렸을 때의 모습을 그대로 연상케 해준다. 다시 말하자면, 殉教者 예수의 모습과 동일한 imagery이다. Santiago의 제 3 의 속성인 martyr를 여기서 볼 수 있다. 좀 더 자세한 解說을 위해선 拙著 〈研究〉 p.228 및 Melvin Backman "The Matador and the Crucified", *Hemingway and His Critics*, ed. Carlos Baker (New York: Hill and Wang, Inc., 1961), p.256을 보라.
* **crying** : 소년은 断腸의 슬픔을 느끼지만 그 감정을 표현한 이 작가는 'cry'를 네군데에 사용하여 objective correlative의 理論을 導用하고 있다. (拙著 〈研究〉 pp.172–173 및 李昌培 "The Objective Correlative" 〈영어영문학〉 제 9 집, 1960, 참조).

The boy did not go down. He had been there before and one of the fishermen was looking after the skiff for him.

"How is he?" one of the fishermen shouted.

"Sleeping," the boy called. He did not care that they saw him crying. "Let no one disturb him."

"He was eighteen feet from nose to tail," the fisherman who was measuring him called.

"I believe it," the boy said.

He went into the Terrace and asked for a can of coffee.

"Hot and with plenty of milk and sugar in it."

"Anything more?"

"No. Afterwards I will see what he can eat."

"What a fish it was," the proprietor said. "There has never been such a fish. Those were two fine fish you took yesterday too."

"Damn my fish," the boy said and he started to cry again.

"Do you want a drink of any kind?" the proprietor asked.

"No," the boy said. "Tell them not to bother Santiago. I'll be back."

"Tell him how sorry I am."

"Thanks," the boy said.

The boy carried the hot can of coffee up to the old man's shack and sat by him until he woke.

Once it looked as though he were waking. But he had gone back into heavy sleep and the boy had gone across the road to borrow some wood to heat the coffee.

Finally the old man woke.

"Don't sit up," the boy said. "Drink this." He poured some of the coffee in a glass.

The old man took it and drank it.

"They beat me, Manolin," he said. "They truly beat me."

"*He* didn't beat you. Not the fish[*]."

"No. Truly. It was afterwards[*]."

"Pedrico[*] is looking after the skiff and the gear. What do you want done with the head?"

"Let Pedrico chop it up to use in fish traps."

"And the spear[*]?"

"You keep it if you want it."

"I want it," the boy said. "Now we must make our plans about the other things."

"Did they search for me?"

"Of course. With coast guard and with planes."

---

* **not the fish** : Fish did not beat you.
* **It was afterwards.** : 「그건 나중이야」.
* **Martin (the proprietor of the Terrace) and Pedrico** : ***A Farewell To Arms*** 의 bartender 의 연장이라 함은 여기서의 例文으로 쉽사리 알 수 있다.
* **the spear** : 「창 같은 주둥이」.

"The ocean is very big and a skiff is small and hard to see," the old man said. He noticed how pleasant it was to have someone to talk to instead of speaking only to himself and to the sea. "I missed you," he said. "What did you catch?"

"One the first day. One the second and two the third."

"Very good."

"Now we fish together again."

"No. I am not lucky. I am not lucky anymore."

"The hell with luck*," the boy said. "I'll bring the luck with me."

"What will your family say?"

"I do not care. I caught two yesterday. But we will fish together now for I still have much to learn*."

"We must get a good killing lance and always have it on board. You can make the blade from a spring leaf from an old Ford.* We can grind it in Guanabacoa.* It should be sharp and not tempered so it will break.* My knife broke."

"I'll get another knife and have the spring ground.

* **The hell with luck.** :「제기랄 운이 다 뭐예요」.
* **I still have much to learn.** : Santiago라는 人物 속에 담겨진 제 2 의 屬性인 apostle적 성격은 이처럼 소년의 태도를 통해 표현된다. 그것은 마치 예수의 사도 Santiago (St. James)가 예수에게서 배운 진리를 세상 사람들에게 가르친 것을 연상케 해준다.
* **an old Ford** :「낡은 포오드 자동차」.
* **Guanabacoa** : Cuba의 도시명.

How many days of heavy *brisa* have we?"

"Maybe three. Maybe more."

"I will have everything in order," the boy said. "You get your hands*well old man."

"I know how to care for them. In the night I spat something strange and felt something in my chest was broken."

"Get that well too," the boy said. "Lie down, old man, and I will bring you your clean shirt. And something to eat."

"Bring any of the papers of the time that I was gone," the old man said.

"You must get well fast for there is much that I can learn and you can teach me everything. How much did you suffer?"

"Plenty," the old man said.

"I'll bring the food and the papers," the boy said. "Rest well, old man. I will bring stuff*from the drugstore for your hands."

"Don't forget to tell Pedrico the head is his."

"No. I will remember."

As the boy went out the door and down the worn coral rock road he was crying again.

---

* **You get your hands well.**: 「손이나 잘 치료해 두어라」. get ~ well: 「고치다, 회복하다」.
* **not tempered so it will break** : It should not be tempered so that it will break.; It should be tempered so that it may not break.
* **stuff** : medicine.

That afternoon there was a party of tourists at the Terrace and looking down in the water among the empty beer cans and dead barracudas a woman saw a great long white spine with a huge tail at the end that lifted and swung with the tide while the east wind blew a heavy steady sea outside the entrance to the harbour.

"What's that?" she asked a waiter and pointed to the long backbone of the great fish that was now just garbage waiting to go out with the tide.

"Tiburon*," the waiter said. "Eshark*." He was meaning to explain what had happened.

"I didn't know sharks had such handsome, beautifully formed tails."

"I didn't either*," her male companion said.

Up the road, in his shack, the old man was sleeping again. He was still sleeping on his face and the boy was sitting by him watching him. The old man was dreaming about the lions*.

---

* **Tiburon** : 상어의 일종.
* **Eshark** : A shark. 영어를 모르는 보이가 그렇게 말한 것.
* **I didn't either.**: I didn't know sharks had such handsome, beautifully formed tails either. 「나도 그렇소」.
* **lions** : 이 작품은 노인이 사자꿈을 꾸는 것으로 끝맺고 있다. 이것은 결국 이 작품의 主題意識이 虛無가 아니라 肯定이라는 것을 의미한다. givers of strength and purity의 symbol인 lions를 꿈꾼다는 것은 희망을 미래에다 걸고 실패에 꺾이지 않고 다시 한번 준비를 갖춰가지고 재도전하겠다는 굳은 결의의 표명이다.

ESSAYS IN CRITICISM

Hemingway's Ambiguity : Symbolism and Irony

by E. M. Halliday

I

One of the curious things about *The Old Man and the Sea* was the sense of awe that it created in its author, its publisher, and (to judge by many of the reviewers) its readers. "Don't you think it is a strange damn story that it should affect all of us (me especially) the way it does?" [1] wrote Hemingway to one of *Life*'s editors. And Scribner's dust jacket responded like a good Greek chorus, "One cannot hope to explain why the reading of this book is so profound an experience." [2]

There has always been a certain mystery about Hemingway's effects in his best writing. From *In Our Time* (1925), with its puzzling "chapters" connecting (or separating) the stories, through *For Whom the Bell Tolls* (1940), with its oddly equivocal interpretation of the Spanish civil war, his best has evoked a somewhat doubtful sound from critics who nevertheless were at pains to recommend. Something, it was felt, was being missed; or if not missed, then sensed too vaguely for critical description. *A Farewell to Arms* (1929), declared Edward Hope in the New York *Herald Tribune*, was "one of those things—like the Grand Canyon—that one doesn't care to talk about." [3] Despite such reverent throwing up of hands by early critics many things were aptly observed; but the emphasis was heavily on Hemingway the realist, whose bright fidelity to the perceptible surfaces of life was accomplished through living dialogue and a prose finely engineered to the accurate rendering of sensuous experience. And the brilliance of his reflected surface together with the roughness of the things he preferred to write about—fishing, hunting, skiing, bullfighting, boxing, horse-racing, and war—perhaps made it

[1] Quoted in *Time*, LX, No. 9 (Sept. 1, 1952), 48.

[2] *The Old Man and the Sea* (New York: Scribner, 1952).

[3] Quoted on the flyleaf of *A Farewell to Arms*, Bantam Edition (New York, 1954).

difficult to see one of the cardinal facts about Hemingway: that essentially he is a philosophical writer. His main interest, in representing human life through fictional forms, has consistently been to set man against the background of his world and universe, to examine the human situation from various points of view.

Not that he has a "system," for on the final questions Hemingway has always shown himself a skeptic. "It seemed like a fine philosophy," Jake Barnes says to himself at one bitter point in *The Sun Also Rises.* "In five years . . . it will seem just as silly as all the other fine philosophies I've had." [4] Like Jake, Hemingway has been "technically" a Roman Catholic, but the metaphysical doctrines of Christianity seem never to have taken a convincing hold. His most devout characters are only devoutly mystified by the universe: both Anselmo, the good old man of *For Whom the Bell Tolls,* and Santiago, of *The Old Man and the Sea;* disclaim their religiosity, and their Hail-Marys are uttered mechanically enough to evoke a chilly memory of the sleepless waiter in "A Clean, Well-Lighted Place," who prayed, "Hail nothing, full of nothing, nothing is with thee." [5] The parable of the doomed ants on the burning log, in *A Farewell to Arms,*[6] has been thought to represent Hemingway's *Weltanschauung* at its most pessimistic; but there is no reason, actually, to think that there has since been a fundamental change in his view of life. "Everything kills everything else in some way," [7] reflects the old Cuban fisherman of the latest book; and even the small bird that rests momentarily on his fishing line may fall to the hawks before reaching land, at best must take its chance "like any man or bird or fish." [8] The world, it seems, still breaks everyone, and only the earth and the Gulf Stream abide after the vortex of human vanities has subsided forever.

Given Hemingway's suspicion of ultimate doom and his passionate fondness for being alive, it is no surprise that his philosophical preoccupation is primarily ethical. Extinction may well be the end of all, as the writer of Ecclesiastes repeatedly remarked, but for Hemingway and his heroes this merely emphasizes the need to live each moment properly and skilfully, to sense judiciously the texture of every fleeting act and perception. The focus is conduct: "Maybe if you found out how to live in it you learned from that what it was all about," [9] says Jake Barnes. It is not accidental that the French existentialists have shown a strong feeling for Hemingway's work. Like them he has been poised in his hours of despair on the edge of nothingness, the abyss of nonmeaning

[4] *The Sun Also Rises* (New York: Scribner, 1926), p. 153.
[5] *The Short Stories of Ernest Hemingway* (New York: Scribner, 1938), p. 481.
[6] *A Farewell to Arms* (New York: Scribner, 1932), p. 350.
[7] *The Old Man and the Sea,* p. 117.
[8] *Ibid.,* p. 61.
[9] *The Sun Also Rises,* p. 153.

which confronts most of the characters in the stories of *Winner Take Nothing* (1933); and like them he has looked in his hours of hope to a salvation built out of individual human courage around a code, at once rational and intuitive, of strict, often ritualistic behavior. "*Nous sommes foutus . . . comme toujours,*" says Golz, the Loyalist general commanding the attack with which Jordan's mission is co-ordinated in *For Whom the Bell Tolls*. "*. . . Bon. Nous ferons notre petit possible.*" [10] As it was for Socrates and Jeremy Taylor, although for quite different reasons, dying well is for Hemingway the crucial corollary to living well. So Robert Jordan fights off an impulse to kill himself to end the anguish of a badly broken leg and avoid possible capture. "You can do nothing for yourself but perhaps you can do something for another," [11] he tells himself; yet we are to understand that he has died well not just because of his sacrifice, but because he has not abandoned the principle of fortitude. In the image of the crucifixion which has haunted Hemingway from "Today Is Friday" (1926) to *The Old Man and the Sea*, it is the unique courage of the forsaken and crucified man-God that takes his attention. "I'll tell you," says a Roman soldier in the earlier work, "he looked pretty good to me in there today." [12] We are part of a universe offering no assurance beyond the grave, and we are to make what we can of life by a pragmatic ethic spun bravely out of man himself in full and steady cognizance that the end is darkness.

II

Undoubtedly Hemingway's preoccupation with the human predicament and a moral code that might satisfactorily control it, in itself partly accounts for the sense of hidden significance which many have experienced in reading him. Obscured as this preoccupation has been by his choice of particular fictional materials and by his manner, which has always eschewed explication, it could nevertheless almost always be felt: it was impossible to avoid the impression that this writer was dealing with something of final importance to us all. Like the Elizabethans whom he evidently loves, he never lets us quite forget that death awaits every man at some turn perhaps not far along the way. And like nobody but Hemingway—that is, in his peculiar and distinguished manner as an artist—he continually reminds us that (as he expressed it once to Maxwell Perkins) it is our "performance en route" [13] that counts for good or bad.

But what is the essence of his peculiar manner? It is a manner of implication, clearly, as he himself has said in various notes of self-

[10] *For Whom the Bell Tolls* (New York: Scribner, 1940), pp. 428, 430.
[11] *Ibid.*, p. 466.
[12] *The Short Stories*, p. 457.
[13] Quoted by Perkins in *Scribner's Magazine*, LXXXI (March, 1927),

criticism of which the figure in *Death in the Afternoon* is perhaps the most striking: "The dignity of movement of an ice-berg is due to only one-eighth of it being above water." [14] The question is what mode of narrative technique he exploits in order to make the ice-berg principle operative in his work. I do not remember seeing the word "symbolism" in critical writing about Hemingway before 1940, nor have I seen more than one review of *The Old Man and the Sea* that did not lean heavily on the word. The number of exegeses that explain Hemingway as a symbolist has increased geometrically since Malcolm Cowley suggested in 1944 that he should be grouped not among the realists, but "with Poe and Hawthorne and Melville: the haunted and nocturnal writers, the men who dealt in images that were symbols of an inner world." [15] It was a startling and pleasing suggestion. Mr. Cowley advanced it rather tentatively and did not press his discovery very far; but it was taken up with something like a hue and cry by other critics who, it seemed, had been testily waiting for the scent and were eager to get on with the hunt. Literary conversation soon began to reflect the new trend: I recall hearing it asserted on two proximate occasions that the sleeping bag in *For Whom the Bell Tolls* is an "obvious" symbol of the womb; and that a ketchup bottle in "The Killers" patently symbolizes blood. By 1949 it was no great surprise to open an issue of the *Sewanee Review* to an essay by Caroline Gordon called "Notes on Hemingway and Kafka." [16] It would have been surprising only if the analysis had not hinged on a comparison between the two writers as symbolists.

Is Hemingway genuinely a symbolist? I think he uses certain techniques of symbolism, but I think he does so in a very limited and closely controlled way, and that failure to recognize the controls leads—already has led—to distortions of his meaning and misappreciations of his narrative art. As a sample, Miss Gordon's essay is instructive on this point. Starting calmly, as her title suggests, with the assumption that Hemingway is a symbolist, she proceeds to compare him, not very favorably, with Kafka. And it turns out that Hemingway's trouble is simple—he is not *enough* of a symbolist: "this plane of action is for him a slippery sub-stratum glimpsed intermittently. It does not underlie the Naturalistic plane of action solidly, or over-arch it grandly, as Kafka's Symbolism does." [17]

But this is mistaking an artistic discipline for a fault. Hemingway has not attempted Kafka's kind of symbolism and fallen short: it is something foreign to Hemingway's art. The Kafka story used by Miss Gordon as the basis for her comparison is "The Hunter Gracchus," a carefully elaborated allegory revolving around the life of Christ—that

[14] *Death in the Afternoon* (New York: Scribner, 1932), p. 192.
[15] Introduction to *The Portable Hemingway* (New York: Viking, 1944), p. vii.
[16] *Sewanee Review*, LVII (Spring, 1949), 214-226.
[17] *Ibid.*, p. 226.

is to say, there are two distinct and parallel narrative lines, the primary, which operates within the confines of a more or less realistic world, and the secondary, which operates within the realm of religious myth and in this case is assumed by the author to be a prior possession on the part of the reader. Incidentally, Miss Gordon forces her comparison from both sides, claiming for Kafka, as something he shares with Hemingway, "a surface which is strictly Naturalistic in detail." [18] But this claim must rest on a curious understanding of the phrase "in detail" since the story on the "Naturalistic" level offers, among other attractions, a corpse that is mysteriously still alive, and a German-speaking dove the size of a rooster.

Hemingway, as far as I know, has never written an allegory—notwithstanding the bright interpretations of *The Old Man and the Sea* that illuminated cocktail parties a few years ago when it was published in *Life*—and for a very good reason. In successful allegory, the story on the primary level is dominated by the story on the secondary level, and if the allegorical meaning is to be kept clear, its naturalistic counterpart must pay for it by surrendering realistic probability in one way or another. A strain is imposed on the whole narrative mechanism, for mere connotative symbolism will not do to carry the allegory: there must be a denotative equation, part for part, between symbols and things symbolized in order to identify the actors and action on the allegorical level. The extreme difficulty of satisfactorily conducting the dual action throughout a prolonged narrative is classically illustrated by *The Faerie Queene* and by *The Pilgrim's Progress*. The allegorist who admires realism is constantly pulled in two directions at once, and is very lucky when he can prevent one or the other of his meanings from unbalancing him.

Still, Hemingway has used the symbolism of association to convey by implication his essential meaning from the time of his earliest American publication. It may well be that this was inevitable for a writer starting out with Hemingway's determination to communicate, as he put it (in *Death in the Afternoon*) "what really happened in action; what the actual things were which produced the emotion that you experienced." [19] Nothing could more clearly differentiate Hemingway's kind of realism from Zolaesque naturalistic description than this early statement of intent. Everything is to depend on judicious discrimination of objective details: *what really happened* is not by any means everything that happened; it is only "the actual things . . . which produced the emotion that you experienced." As a matter of fact "produced" is a little too strict, as Hemingway demonstrates again and again in *The Sun Also Rises* and *A Farewell to Arms*, where he depends heavily on the technique of objective epitome—a symbolist technique, if you like—to con-

[18] *Ibid.*, p. 222.

[19] *Death in the Afternoon*, p. 2.

vey the subjective conditions of his characters. The details selected are not so much those which *produce* the emotion as those which epitomize it; it is the action of the story which has produced the emotion. Thus at the crisis of *The Sun Also Rises,* when Jake Barnes presents Brett to Pedro Romero—a Pandarism for which he is obliged to hate himself —his agonized feelings are not discussed, but are nevertheless most poignantly suggested by the perceptions he reports:

> When I came back and looked in the café, twenty minutes later, Brett and Pedro Romero were gone. The coffee-glasses and our three empty cognac-glasses were on the table. A waiter came with a cloth and picked up the glasses and mopped off the table.[20]

In *A Farewell to Arms,* Frederic Henry goes dully out for breakfast from the Swiss maternity hospital where Catherine Barkley is fighting for life in ominously abnormal labor:

> Outside along the street were the refuse cans from the houses waiting for the collector. A dog was nosing at one of the cans.
>
> "What do you want?" I asked and looked in the can to see if there was anything I could pull out for him; there was nothing on top but coffee-grounds, dust and some dead flowers.
>
> "There isn't anything, dog," I said.[21]

There is, of course, a larger sense, germane to all good fiction, in which Hemingway may be said to be symbolic in his narrative method: the sense which indicates his typical creation of key characters who are representative on several levels. We thus find Jake Barnes's war-wound impotence a kind of metaphor for the whole atmosphere of sterility and frustration which is the *ambiance* of *The Sun Also Rises*; we find Catherine Barkley's naïve simplicity and warmth the right epitome for the idea and ideal of normal civilian home life to which Frederic Henry deserts; we find the old Cuban fisherman in some way representative of the whole human race in its natural struggle for survival. But the recent criticism of Hemingway as symbolist goes far beyond such palpable observations as these, and in considering the fundamental character of his narrative technique I wish to turn attention to more ingenious if not esoteric explications.

Professor Carlos Baker, in *Hemingway: The Writer as Artist* (1952), has established himself as the leading oracle of Hemingway's symbolism. His book is, I think, the most valuable piece of extended Hemingway criticism that we yet have, and to a large extent its contribution is one of new insights into the symbolist aspect of his subject's narrative method. He is sweeping:

[20] *The Sun Also Rises*, p. 194.
[21] *A Farewell to Arms*, p. 336.

> From the first Hemingway has been dedicated as a writer to the rendering of *Wahrheit*, the precise and at least partly naturalistic rendering of things as they are and were. Yet under all his brilliant surfaces lies the controlling *Dichtung*, the symbolic underpainting which gives so remarkable a sense of depth and vitality to what otherwise might be flat two-dimensional portraiture.[22]

This may fairly be said to represent Mr. Baker's major thesis, and he develops and supports it with remarkable energy and skill. I do not wish to disparage his over-all effort—he is often very enlightening—but I do wish to argue that he has been rather carried away by his thesis, and that therein he eminently typifies the new symbolist criticism of Hemingway which in its enthusiasm slights or ignores other basic aspects of Hemingway's technique.

Mr. Baker's chapter on *A Farewell to Arms* is an original piece of criticism, and it solidly illustrates his approach. He finds that the essential meaning of this novel is conveyed by two master symbols, the Mountain and the Plain, which organize the *Dichtung* around "two poles":

> By a process of accrual and coagulation, the images tend to build round the opposed concepts of Home and Not-Home. . . . The Home-concept, for example, is associated with the mountains; with dry-cold weather; with peace and quiet; with love, dignity, health, happiness, and the good life; and with worship or at least the consciousness of God. The Not-Home concept is associated with low-lying plains; with rain and fog; with obscenity, indignity, disease, suffering, nervousness, war and death; and with irreligion.[23]

It is in terms of these antipodal concepts that Mr. Baker analyzes the semantic structure of *A Farewell to Arms*, a structure which he finds effective chiefly because of the adroit and subtle development of the correspondingly antipodal symbols, the Mountain and the Plain. He argues that from the first page of the story these are set up in their significant antithesis, that they are the key to the relationships among several of the leading characters, and that the central action—Frederic Henry's desertion from the Italian Army to join Catherine Barkley, the British nurse—can be fully appreciated only on this symbolic basis. "*A Farewell to Arms*," he concludes, "is entirely and even exclusively acceptable as a naturalistic narrative of what happened. To read it only as such, however, is to miss the controlling symbolism: the deep central antithesis between the image of life and home (the mountain) and the image of war and death (the plain)." [24]

[22] Carlos Baker, *Hemingway: The Writer as Artist* (Princeton: Princeton University Press, 1952), p. 289.

[23] *Ibid.*, pp. 101, 102.

[24] *Ibid.*, pp. 108, 109.

Clearly there is some truth in this. The "deep central antithesis" cannot be denied, I would think, by anyone with an acceptable understanding of the book. The question at issue is one of technique; to what extent, and how precisely, is the central antithesis in fact engineered around the Mountain and the Plain as symbols?

One thing is noticeable immediately: as in virtually all of Hemingway, anything that can possibly be construed to operate symbolically does no violence whatsoever to the naturalism (or realism) of the story on the primary level. Nothing could be a more natural—or more traditional—symbol of purity, of escape from the commonplace, in short of elevation, than mountains. If thousands of people have read the passages in *A Farewell to Arms* which associate the mountains "with dry-cold weather; with peace and quiet; with love, dignity, health, happiness and the good life" without taking them to be "symbolic" it is presumably because these associations are almost second nature for all of us. Certainly this seems to be true of Frederic Henry: it is most doubtful that in the course of the novel he is ever to be imagined as consciously regarding the mountains as a symbol. This of course does not prove that Hemingway did not regard them as such, or that the full understanding of this novel as an art structure does not perhaps require the symbolic equation, *mountain* equals *life and home*. It does, however, point differentially to another type of symbolism, where the character in question is shown to be clearly aware of the trope, as when Catherine Barkley says she hates rain because "sometimes I see me dead in it," [25] or when Frederic Henry says of his plunge into the Tagliamento, "Anger was washed away in the river along with any obligation." [26]

But Mr. Baker has claimed a most exact and detailed use by Hemingway of the Mountain-Plain symbolism, and his ingenious interpretation deserves closer attention. Like many other critics he is an intense admirer of the novel's opening paragraph, which, he says, "does much more than start the book. It helps to establish the dominant mood (which is one of doom), plants a series of important images for future symbolic cultivation, and subtly compels the reader into the position of detached observer." [27] He proceeds to a close analysis of this paragraph:

> The second sentence, which draws attention from the mountainous background to the bed of the river in the middle distance, produces a sense of clearness, dryness, whiteness, and sunniness which is to grow very subtly under the artist's hands until it merges with one of the novel's two dominant symbols, the mountain-image. The other major symbol is the plain. Throughout the sub-structure of the book it is opposed to the mountain-image. Down this plain the river flows. Across it, on the dusty road among

[25] *A Farewell to Arms*, p. 135.
[26] *Ibid.*, p. 248.
[27] Baker, *op. cit.*, p. 94.

> the trees, pass the men-at-war, faceless and voiceless and unidentified against the background of the spreading plain.[28]

This is highly specific, and we are entitled to examine it minutely. Mr. Baker says the river is "in the middle distance" in the direction of the mountains with the image of which, as he sees it, the symbolic images of the river are to merge into one great symbol. But is the river really in the middle distance? The narrator tells us he can see not only its boulders but its *pebbles,* "dry and white in the sun." The river must, of course, flow from the mountains, but in the perspective seen from the house occupied by Frederic Henry, it would appear to be very close at hand—closer than the plain, and quite in contrast to the distant mountains. And this raises the question of whether the clearness, dryness, whiteness, and sunniness offered by the river are in fact artfully intended to be associated with the mountain-image and what it is held to symbolize; or, disregarding the question of intent, whether they do in fact so operate in the artistic structure. Why must the river images be dissociated from the images of the plain across which the river, naturally, flows? Because the river images are of a kind which, if they work as symbols, are incongruent with what Mr. Baker has decided the Plain stands for; they must instead be allocated to the Mountain. This is so important to his thesis that the river shifts gracefully, but without textual support, into "the middle distance," closer to the mountains.

And what of the soldiers on the road? Since they must be firmly associated with the Plain ("war and death"), it is against that background that Mr. Baker sees them in Hemingway's opening paragraph—it would not do to see them against the background of the river, with its Mountain images. But let us look again at the paragraph.

> In the late summer of that year we lived in a house in a village that looked across the river and the plain to the mountains. In the bed of the river there were pebbles and boulders, dry and white in the sun, and the water was clear and swiftly moving and blue in the channels. Troops went by the house and down the road and the dust they raised powdered the leaves of the trees.

Mr. Baker says the road is across the river, as of course it would have to be if we are to see the figures of the soldiers against the background of the plain. Hemingway does not say the road is across the river. Indeed, everything indicates the opposite arrangement: a house on a road running along the near side of the river, across which the plain stretches out to the mountains. "Sometimes in the dark," begins the third paragraph of the novel, "we heard the troops marching under the window. . . ."

[28] *Ibid.*, pp. 94-95.

The truth is that a strong part of Mr. Baker's initially persuasive exegesis of the opening paragraph of *A Farewell to Arms* hangs on a reading that the written words will not support. This is not to deny that the paragraph establishes a mood of doom by its somber tone and the epitomic symbols of dust and falling leaves: what I am questioning is the over-all symbolic organization of the novel's structure in terms of the Mountain and the Plain, which Mr. Baker argues as a prime illustration of his unequivocal judgment of Hemingway as symbolist artist.

As a matter of fact, the plain presented in the opening pages of *A Farewell to Arms* is as troublesome as the river when it comes to supporting Mr. Baker's interpretation. There are plains in many countries that could well serve as symbols of emptiness, desolation, disaster, and death—we have some in the American West. But this does not appear to be that sort of plain: quite the contrary. "The plain," Frederic Henry narrates in the opening words of the second paragraph, "was rich with crops; there were many orchards of fruit trees. . . ." Mr. Baker tells us neither how these images of fertility and fruition are to fit in with "rain and fog; with obscenity, indignity, disease, suffering, nervousness, war and death," nor how we should symbolically interpret the conclusion of the sentence, ". . . and beyond the plain the mountains were brown and bare." One can easily grant that as the novel unfolds, the impression of war itself grows steadily more saturated with a sense of doomsday qualities: that was an essential part of Hemingway's theme. But to what degree is this impression heightened by the use of the Plain as symbol? The simple exigencies of history prevent exclusive association of the war with the plain as opposed to the mountains, as the narrator indicates on the first page: "There was fighting in the mountains and at night we could see flashes from the artillery." Yet if Mr. Baker is right we would expect to find, despite this difficulty, a salient artistic emphasis of the Plain in symbolic association with all those images which his interpretation sets against those coalescing around the Mountain symbol.

Mr. Baker makes much of the fact that Frederic Henry, during his leave, fails to take advantage of the offer of his friend the chaplain and go to the high mountain country of the Abruzzi, "where the roads were frozen and hard as iron, where it was clear cold and dry and the snow was dry and powdery. . . . I had gone to no such place but to the smoke of cafés and nights when the room whirled and you needed to look at the wall to make it stop, nights in bed, drunk, when you knew that that was all there was."[29] Here, Mr. Baker claims, "the mountain-image gets further backing from another lowland contrast."[30]

[29] *A Farewell to Arms*, p. 13.

[30] Baker, *op. cit.*, p. 102.

Granting the familiar association here of mountain-country with certain delectable and longed-for experiences, one would like to see, in support of the Mountain-Plain explication, a clearer identification of the contrasting, soldier-on-leave experiences, with the lowland or plain. And while wondering about this, one reads on in *A Farewell to Arms* and soon finds Frederic Henry and Catherine Barkley in Milan, where Henry is recuperating from his wound. They are having a wonderful time. They are in love, have frequent opportunities to be alone together in the hospital room, go often to the races, dine at the town's best restaurants, and in general lead an existence that makes the most pleasant contrast imaginable to the dismal life at the front. "We had a lovely time that summer," [31] says the hero. What has happened here to the Mountain-Plain machinery? It does not seem to be operating; or perhaps it is operating in reverse, since Milan is definitely in the plain. Mr. Baker passes over these pages of the novel rather quickly, remarking that Catherine here "moves into association with ideas of home, love and happiness." [32] He seems to be aware of the difficulty, although he does not mention it as such: "She does not really [*sic*] reach the center of the mountain-image until, on the heels of Frederic's harrowing lowland experiences during the retreat from Caporetto, the lovers move to Switzerland. Catherine is the first to go, and Henry follows her there as if she were the genius of the mountains, beckoning him on." [33]

This is romantically pleasant, but inaccurate. Catherine does not go to Switzerland, but to the Italian resort village of Stresa, on Lake Maggiore. Stresa, moreover, although surrounded by mountains, is itself distinctly lowland: you can pedal a bicycle from Milan or Turin without leaving nearly flat country. Still, it can be allowed that the lovers are not free of the contaminating shadow of war until they have escaped up the lake to Switzerland and established themselves in their little chalet above Montreux. Here, again, the associations all of us are likely to make with high-mountain living assert themselves—clear, cold air; magnificent views; white snow; peace and quiet—and the hero and heroine are shown to be happily aware of these. The rain, however, which they have both come to regard as an omen of disaster, grants no immunity to the mountain; it refuses to preserve a unilateral symbolic association with the plain. Mr. Baker knows this, but does not discuss the extent to which it obscures his neat Mountain-Plain antithesis, making the point instead that "the March rains and the approaching need for a good lying-in hospital have driven the young couple down from their magic mountain" to "the lowlands" [34] of Lausanne. Here again

[31] *A Farewell to Arms*, p. 119.
[32] Baker, *op. cit.*, p. 104.
[33] *Ibid.*
[34] *Ibid.*, pp. 104, 108.

observation is fuzzy to the point of distortion: Lausanne happens to stand on a series of steep hills and is an extraordinarily poor specimen of a City of the Plain. This is clear, incidentally, without reference to an atlas, since there are several allusions to the hills and steep streets of Lausanne in the novel itself.[35] But Mr. Baker is caught up in his symbolic apparatus, and if one symbol of death (rain) has failed to stay where it belongs in his scheme (on the plain) he still is persuaded to see the topography of Switzerland in a light that will not darken his thesis.

What all this illustrates, it seems to me, is that Mr. Baker has allowed an excellent insight into Hemingway's imagery and acute sense of natural metonymy to turn into an interesting but greatly overelaborated critical gimmick. It is undeniable that in the midst of the darkling plain of struggle and flight which was the war in Italy, Frederic Henry thinks of the Swiss Alps as a neutral refuge of peace and happiness—surely millions must have lifted their eyes to those mountains with like thoughts during both World Wars. But in so far as this is symbolism it belongs to our race and culture; and if it is to be sophisticated into a precise scheme of artistic implication revolving around two distinct polar symbols, the signals transmitted from artist to reader must be more clearly semaphored than anything Mr. Baker has been able to point to accurately. I do not believe this is derogatory to Hemingway. Sensitive as always to those parts of experience that are suggestive and connotative, he used the mountain metaphor which is part of our figurative heritage to deepen the thematic contrast in *A Farewell to Arms,* between war and not-war. But nowhere did he violate realism for the sake of this metaphor; nor did he, as I read the novel, set up the artificially rigid and unrealistic contrast between the Mountain and the Plain which Mr. Baker's analysis requires.

Mr. Baker himself has summed up the sequel to his investigation of *A Farewell to Arms.* "Once the reader has become aware of what Hemingway is doing in those parts of his work which lie below the surface, he is likely to find symbols operating everywhere. . . ." [36] Mr. Baker does find them everywhere, and they not infrequently trip him into strangely vulnerable judgments. Finding an unprecedented display of symbolism in *Across the River and Into the Trees* (1950), for instance, he is willing to accord that disappointing novel a richly favorable verdict: "a prose poem, with a remarkably complex emotional structure, on the theme of the three ages of man. . . . If *A Farewell to Arms* was his *Romeo and Juliet* . . . this . . . could perhaps be called a lesser kind of *Winter's Tale* or *Tempest.*" [37]

[35] See, for instance, pp. 328, 331, 334.
[36] Baker, *op. cit.,* p. 117.
[37] *Ibid.,* pp. 264, 287.

III

But we are not interested so much in the narrative technique of Hemingway's weakest work as we are in what happens in his best. To see symbolism as the master device of the earlier novels and short stories tends to obscure another and more characteristic type of ambiguity which makes his best work great fiction in the tacit mode. I mean Hemingway's irony. The extent to which the ironic method has packed his fiction with substrata of meaning has not yet, I think, been adequately appreciated in published criticism. And it needs to be appreciated; for irony as a literary device is singularly suited to the view of life which Hemingway has consistently dramatized now for a quarter of our century in such manner as to distinguish him as a writer.

If you look at Hemingway's earliest American publication in a medium of general circulation you are struck by this irony of view and method, just as it is strikingly there in *The Old Man and the Sea.* "Champs d'Honneur" was the title of one of six short poems printed in *Poetry* for January, 1923:

Soldiers never do die well;
  Crosses mark the places—
Wooden crosses where they fell,
  Stuck above their faces.
Soldiers pitch and cough and twitch—
  All the world roars red and black;
Soldiers smother in a ditch,
  Choking through the whole attack.[38]

One of the most interesting things about this is the strong ironic tension set up between the title and the verse itself; the harsh incongruity between the traditional notion of the soldier's heroic death and the grim reality. A tough irony of situation is also the keynote of *In Our Time* (1925), not only as clue to the individual meanings of most of the stories that make up the book, but as the very principle upon which it was composed. Many readers have tried to puzzle out a nice relationship between each story and the narrative fragment, numbered as a "chapter," which precedes it. But the principle in fact was irrelevance; what Hemingway did was to take the numbered sketches of *in our time* (Paris, 1924) and intersperse them with the longer stories to give a powerfully ironic effect of spurious order supporting the book's subject: modern civil disruption and violence seen against the timeless background of everyday human cross-purposes.

[38] *Poetry*, XXI (January, 1923), 195.

The ironic gap between expectation and fulfillment, pretense and fact, intention and action, the message sent and the message received, the way things are thought or ought to be and the way things are—this has been Hemingway's great theme from the beginning; and it has called for an ironic method to do it artistic justice. All of his work thus far published deserves study with special attention to this method.

I do not think, for example, that a reader must understand the symbolic pattern Mr. Baker claims for *A Farewell to Arms* in order to get the main point of the story; but unless he understands the irony of Catherine Barkley's death he surely has missed it completely. Long before this denouement, however, irony has drawn a chiaroscuro highlighting the meaning of the book. There is from the beginning the curious disproportion between Frederic Henry's lot in the army and his frame of mind. A noncombatant, he lives in comfortable houses, eats and drinks well, makes frequent visits to a brothel maintained exclusively for officers, and has extensive leaves urged on him by a sympathetic commanding officer. Despite such pleasures he is malcontent; and the more this fact emerges the more it becomes evident that his mood is a reflection not of his personal fortune, but of the whole dismal panorama of civilization disjointed by war. His manner of narration is already ironical: "At the start of the winter came the permanent rain and with the rain came the cholera. But it was checked and in the end only seven thousand died of it in the army." [39] Healthy in body, the hero is afflicted by a paralysis of the will, a torpor brought on by too many months of living close to the war; and this is the reason for his paradoxical failure to visit the home of his friend the chaplain while he is on leave: "I myself felt as badly as he did and could not understand why I had not gone. It was what I had wanted to do. . . ." [40] Even the one constructive effort he has been regularly capable of, the performance of his duty as an ambulance officer, has begun to seem absurdly inconsequential to him: when he returns from leave he finds that his absence apparently has made no difference whatever.

As the war wears on, its grotesqueries receive more attention; it begins to be felt, indeed, that they are perhaps after all indigenous to life itself, and only emphasized by war. Henry is given a protective St. Anthony by the heroine: "After I was wounded I never found him. Some one probably got it at one of the dressing stations." [41] The ambulance unit which he commands makes elaborate preparations to receive wounded soldiers during a forthcoming attack: while they are waiting—and eating cheese and spaghetti—in a dugout, an enemy shell lands squarely on top of them, thus making Lt. Henry himself part

[39] *A Farewell to Arms*, p. 4.
[40] *Ibid.*, p. 13.
[41] *Ibid.*, p. 47.

of the first load of wounded going to the rear. For this, he learns, he is to receive a bronze medal; his friend Rinaldi hopes it may be silver.

The episode in Milan, so recalcitrant to Mr. Baker's symbolist scheme, has an integral function in the ironic structure of the narrative. Recuperating far behind the lines, the hero becomes part of the incongruously pleasant civilian scene which always—to the incredulous and bitter astonishment of most combat soldiers—goes on while men die at the front. Yet to add a further ironic twist to this, there is Hemingway's satirical portrait of Ettore, the American-Italian who is a "legitimate hero" in the Italian Army. Not only does he see the social life of wartime Milan as perfectly normal, but it is clear that his view of the war as a whole is the reverse of Henry's: "Believe me, they're fine to have," he says, exhibiting his wound stripes. "I'd rather have them than medals. Believe me, boy, when you get three you've got something." [42]

Back at the front for only two days, Henry finds himself mixed up in the nightmarish retreat from Caporetto. Hemingway's famous description of this debacle is a stringent comment on the bewildering stupidity and chaos of war, but he takes the occasion to inject again a shot of special irony. With one ambulance mired to the hubs on a rainsoaked back road, Lt. Henry shoots a sergeant who, in his anxiety to keep up with the retreat, tries to get away on foot instead of staying to cut brush for the spinning wheels. The sergeant is only wounded, but he is quickly dispatched, with Henry's acquiescence, by Bonello, one of the ambulance drivers. "All my life I've wanted to kill a sergeant," [43] Bonello says proudly; but a few hours later he too deserts, to let himself be captured by the enemy. The climax of this grim comedy is of course Frederic Henry's own desertion. Threatened with military justice akin to that he so summarily had dealt the sergeant, he dives into the Tagliamento River; and his sarcastic remarks on his would-be executioners ring with hyperironic overtones against the baffle of the earlier incident:

> I saw how their minds worked; if they had minds and if they worked. They were all young men and they were saving their country. . . . The questioners had that beautiful detachment and devotion to stern justice of men dealing in death without being in any danger of it.[44]

There are many other ironic strokes in *A Farewell to Arms*, but it is this series, identifying the activities of war with all that is brutal and meaningless in human life, that gives the novel its predominantly ironic texture. The catastrophe, Catherine Barkley's shocking death, has the ambivalent effect of partly canceling this identification while at the

[42] *Ibid.*, p. 130.
[43] *Ibid.*, p. 222.
[44] *Ibid.*, pp. 240, 241.

same time violently reinforcing the total effect of irony. It is as if the author had said, "Do not imagine that the kind of cruelty and disruption I have shown you are confined to war: they are the conditions of life itself." It is thus only at the end that the full ironic ambiguity of the title springs into view.

The title of Hemingway's other great war novel is likewise an index of its strongly ironic theme. It was strange how many reviewers and critics underweighed the epigraph from Donne and the meaningful paradox of the whole sentence furnishing the title: "And therefore never send to know for whom the bell tolls: it tolls for thee." Appraisals from both Right and Left accused Hemingway of having gone over to the other side, while certain critics less politically biased found that his theme was confused or that it had backfired. "At the center of *For Whom the Bell Tolls*," wrote Maxwell Geismar, "there is a basic confusion of Hemingway's intention. The novel attempts to be a constructive statement on human life. Yet Hemingway's underlying sense of destruction often contradicts this." [45]

But Hemingway was not confused. As always, he wanted to show something true about human life (not necessarily something "constructive"); and he had come to take a more complex view of humanity at war than he projected in *A Farewell to Arms*. "A plague on both your houses"—the prevailing mood of Frederic Henry—has been replaced by Robert Jordan's unillusioned sense of the community of the human predicament. No man is an island, it turns out; but the storms that sweep the human continent are of such force, and the quakes that rack its surface so disruptive, that none of us can depend on better fortune that that of Jordan, who died making his own small and paradoxical effort to maintain its integrity. His affiliation with the Loyalists is no simple partisan allegiance; and to extend and support the hero's explicit awareness of the inevitable contradictions of his position, Hemingway poses a series of situations pregnant with irony.

Outstanding is Pilar's account of the start of "the movement" in Pablo's home town, with its unflinching report of the steadily mounting sadism which infused the execution of the local Fascists. There is a remarkable tone to this report, as if Pilar were at confession, anxious to tell the whole truth and omitting not even the most shameful details, yet seeking at the same time to make it understood how these grisly acts could have occurred among normally decent Spanish peasants. She tells how, at first, many of the peasants were sickened by Pablo's plan to flail the Fascists down between a double line of men leading to the edge of a steep cliff. But within the ironic frame of the entire episode, in relation to the book, there are lesser ironies: for it is the cowardly behavior of the Fascists themselves that brings these peasants to a pitch of mob hatred and violence equal to Pablo's inveterate cruelty.

[45] *Writers in Crisis* (Boston: Houghton, 1942), p. 81.

Throughout all this the reader is never allowed to forget that it is the Loyalists who are committing the atrocities described, and that the leaders of the massacre are the very people with whom Jordan is now allied. Robert Penn Warren cites the irony of this, but he suggests that *For Whom the Bell Tolls* is not Hemingway's best novel "primarily because . . . Hemingway does not accept the limitations of his premises . . . the irony . . . runs counter to the ostensible surface direction of the story." [46] So it does—but this is the nature of irony; and this is why it is so valuable to Hemingway in his intense effort to dramatize fully the implications of Donne's epigraph in relation to the ironical self-destruction which is civilized warfare. It is a mistake to think of *For Whom the Bell Tolls* as a document of social optimism in its intent, as opposed to the dark pessimism of Hemingway's earlier books. The darkness is relieved, deliberately, only by a faint existentialist glimmer: the general human enterprise seems very likely to end in failure, but each of us must do what he can—*"Nous ferons notre petit possible."*

It is to this end that the irony of the Loyalist massacre of the Fascists, which early in the book sets the theme of human sacrifice in a highly critical perspective, is complemented by the irony of the denouement. For the central action—the blowing of the bridge—which is responsible for the death of El Sordo, Anselmo, Fernando, and, indeed, Robert Jordan, is rendered a strategic failure by the loose tongues of their comrades behind the lines.

To these two fundamental veins of irony many scenes provide tributary support: three may be cited as exemplary. There is the one in which Jordan reads the letters found in the pockets of a Fascist cavalryman he has just shot, and discovers he is from a Spanish town that Jordan knows well:

> How many is that you have killed? he asked himself. I don't know. Do you think you have a right to kill any one? No. But I have to. . . . But you like the people of Navarra better than those of any other part of Spain. Yes. And you kill them. Yes. . . . Don't you know it is wrong to kill? Yes. But you do it? Yes. And you still believe absolutely that your cause is right? Yes.[47]

This irony of Jordan's self-conscious ambivalence is heightened by juxtapositions of which he knows nothing. In the midst of El Sordo's great last fight, we are suddenly given a decidedly sympathetic portrait of Lt. Berrendo, second in command of the Fascist cavalry. Julian, his best friend, has just been killed by Sordo, and Captain Mora, the blustering officer in command, is shouting blasphemies at the hilltop in

[46] Introduction to *A Farewell to Arms* (New York: Scribner, 1949), p. xxv.
[47] *For Whom the Bell Tolls*, pp. 303-304.

an effort (which carries its own small irony, in view of his imminent death) to prove that no one is left alive up there. Later, after Mora has become El Sordo's "Comrade Voyager," Berrendo reluctantly has his troopers decapitate the dead guerrillas for "proof and identification," and the Fascists start back towards their headquarters:

> Then he thought of Julian, dead on the hill, dead now, tied across a horse there in the first troop, and as he rode down into the dark pine forest, leaving the sunlight behind him on the hill, riding now in the quiet dark of the forest, he started to say a prayer for him again.[48]

At this point Anselmo, watching from a hillside, sees them ride past; and on his way back to the guerrilla cave he crosses El Sordo's hilltop where he finds the headless bodies of his comrades: "As he walked he prayed for the souls of Sordo and of all his band. It was the first time he had prayed since the start of the movement." [49] The episode thus ends in ironic equilibrium, with both sides petitioning Heaven. But we have not yet seen our last of Lt. Berrendo. It is he who looms in the sights of Robert Jordan's machine gun in the last paragraph of the story, lending the finale an ironic depth that protects it from false heroics. For these two young soldiers, preponderant as our sympathy may be for one rather than the other, the same bell tolls. The novel is Hemingway's fullest work so far in scope and artistic realization, and to its fulfillment the ambiguity of irony contributes an essential part.

IV

It would be foolish to argue that the work of any first-rate writer owes its success exclusively or even predominantly to any one narrative artifice. Hemingway has used techniques of symbolism and techniques of irony and used them well; what we want in criticism is an even view of his use of these and other artistic resources that does not exaggerate one at the expense of others. A point deserving great attention and emphasis about this writer is his devotion to the implict rather than the explicit mode: and both symbolism and irony truly serve this artistic purpose. Hemingway, in fact, stirs thought as to the interrelationship of these two kinds of ambiguity. It is remarkable how often they operate together in his stories: an ironic fact, perception, or event on the primary level may epitomize an irony in a broader context, and thus doubly deserve selection and accurate report by the narrator. As an illustration of his early effort to communicate "what really happened in action," Hemingway tells in *Death in the Afternoon* how he worked on the problem of accurately depicting a certain bullfight incident:

[48] *Ibid.*, p. 326.

[49] *Ibid.*, p. 327.

> Waking in the night I tried to remember what it was that seemed just out of my remembering and that was the thing that I had really seen and, finally, remembering all around it, I got it. When he stood up, his face white and dirty and the silk of his breeches opened from waist to knee, it was the dirtiness of the rented breeches, the dirtiness of his slit underwear and the clean, clean, unbearably clean whiteness of the thighbone that I had seen, and it was that which was important.[50]

Clearly, it was the startling irony of the contrast that struck Hemingway here as "important"; but certainly (if not so clearly) there is also the symbolic suggestion of another contrast going far beyond the physical—the ironically pathetic gap, perhaps, between the matador's professional failure and his untouched inner pride which is the subject of "The Undefeated."

In a fictional narrative the double operation, ironic and symbolic, can often be seen more sharply: take *The Old Man and the Sea*, where in effect the same subject is dramatized. The old fisherman's physical triumph in catching the great fish is ironically cut down—or transmuted—into spiritual triumph by the marauding sharks who leave him with only the skeleton of the largest marlin ever seen in Cuba. Without working out the metaphor in precise terms it can be said that the irony of the event itself would hardly be so effective without the broadening and deepening of its implication through symbolic suggestion.

It may be true that all perceptions are reducible finally to perceptions of likeness or perceptions of difference. Perhaps this offers a clue to the effectiveness of both symbolism and irony for a writer who, like Hemingway, makes it his life's business to tell a truth, as he once put it, "truer . . . than anything factual can be."[51] With all his famous skill in writing with his eye upon the object, he understood from the beginning that it was only the object in relationship to other objects and to the observer that really counted: significance is, in short, a matter of likeness and difference. This is to speak broadly; and to apply the generalization to symbolism and irony requires a good deal of qualification. Yet symbolism does depend essentially on likeness, and irony on difference; and as artistic tools both are means of interpreting imaginatively, and with the flexibility of implication, a complex reality. Symbolism signifies through a harmony, irony through a discord; symbolism consolidates, irony complicates; symbolism synthesizes, irony analyzes.

For all of this, I would not like to see Hemingway go down in new literary histories as either "a symbolist" or (less likely, if somewhat more appropriately) "an ironist." Taken at face value the denomination "symbolist" has meanings in the common language of

[50] *Death in the Afternoon*, p. 20.
[51] Introduction to *Men at War* (New York, 1952), p. xi.

criticism that are quite inapplicable to him. But beyond this, Hemingway uses symbolism, as I have tried to show, with a severe restraint that in his good work always staunchly protects his realism. So likewise does he use irony. It is the ambiguity of life itself that Hemingway has sought to render, and if irony has served him peculiarly well it is because he sees life as inescapably ironic. But if we must classify him let us do him justice: with all his skilful use of artistic ambiguity, he remains the great *realist* of twentieth-century American fiction.

Observations on the Style of Ernest Hemingway

by Harry Levin

I

Hemingway's hatred for the profession of letters stems quite obviously from a lover's quarrel. When Richard Gordon is reviled by his dissatisfied wife in *To Have and Have Not,* her most embittered epithet is "you writer." Yet Hemingway's writing abounds in salutes to various fellow writers, from the waitress' anecdote about Henry James in *The Torrents of Spring* to Colonel Cantwell's spiritual affinity with D'Annunzio. And from Nick Adams, who takes Meredith and Chesterton along on fishing trips, to Hemingway himself, who arranges to be interviewed on American literature in *Green Hills of Africa,* his heroes do not shy away from critical discussion. His titles, so often quoted from books by earlier writers, have been so apt that they have all but established a convention. He shows an almost academic fondness, as well as a remarkable flair, for epigraphs: the Colonel dies with a quotation on his lips. Like all of us, Hemingway has been influenced by T. S. Eliot's taste for Elizabethan drama and metaphysical poetry. Thus Hemingway's title, "In Another Country," is borrowed from a passage he elsewhere cites, which he might have found in Marlowe's *Jew of Malta* or possibly in Eliot's "Portrait of a Lady." *A Farewell to Arms,* which echoes Lovelace's title, quotes in passing from Marvell's "To His Coy Mistress," echoed more recently by Robert Penn Warren, which is parodied in *Death in the Afternoon.* Hemingway is no exception to the rule that makes parody the starting point for realistic fiction. Just as Fielding took off from Richardson, so Hemingway takes off from Sherwood Anderson—indeed his first novel, *The Torrents of Spring,* which parodies Anderson's *Dark Laughter,* is explicit in its acknowledgments to *Joseph Andrews.* It has passages, however, which read today like a *pastiche* of the later Hemingway:

> Yogi was worried. There was something on his mind. It was spring, there was no doubt of that now, and he did not want a woman. He had worried about it a lot lately. There was no question about it. He did not want a woman. He couldn't explain it to himself. He had gone to the Public Library and asked for a book the night before. He looked at the librarian. He did not want her. Somehow she meant nothing to him.

A recoil from bookishness, after a preliminary immersion in it, provided Fielding's master, Cervantes, with the original impetus for the novel. In "A Banal Story" Hemingway provides us with his own variation on the theme of *Don Quixote,* where a writer sits reading about romance in a magazine advertisement, while in far-off Madrid a bullfighter dies and is buried. The ironic contrast—romantic preconception exploded by contact with harsh reality—is basic with Hemingway, as it has been with all novelists who have written effectively about war. The realism of his generation reacted, not only against Wilsonian idealism, but against Wilsonian rhetoric. Hence the famous paragraph from the Caporetto episode describing Frederic Henry's embarrassment before such abstract words as "glory" and "honor," which seem to him obscene beside the concrete names of places and numbers of roads. For a Spaniard, Hemingway notes in *Death in the Afternoon,* the abstraction may still have concreteness: honor may be "as real a thing as water, wine, or olive oil." It is not so for us: "All our words from loose using have lost their edge." And "The Gambler, the Nun, and the Radio" brings forward a clinching example: "Liberty, what we believed in, now the name of a Macfadden publication." That same story trails off in a litany which reduces a Marxist slogan to meaninglessness: "the opium of the people" is everything and nothing. Even more desolating, in "A Clean, Well-Lighted Place," is the reduction of the Lord's prayer to nothingness: "Our nada who art in nada . . ." Since words have become inflated and devalued, Hemingway is willing to recognize no values save those which can be immediately felt and directly pointed out. It is his verbal skepticism which leads toward what some critics have called his moral nihilism. Anything serious had better be said with a smile, stranger. The classic echo, "irony and pity," jingles through *The Sun Also Rises* like a singing commercial.

There is something in common between this attitude and the familiar British habit of understatement. "No pleasure in anything if you mouth it too much," says Wilson, the guide in "The Short, Happy Life of Francis Macomber." Yet Jake, the narrator of *The Sun Also Rises,* protests in the name of American garrulity—that the English use fewer words than the Eskimos. Spanish, the language of Hemingway's preference, is at once emotive and highly formal. His Spanish, to judge from *Death in the Afternoon,* is just as ungrammatical as his English. In "The Undefeated" his Spanish bullfighters are made to speak the slang of American prizefighters. Americanisms and Hispanisms, archaic and polyglot elements are so intermingled in *For Whom the Bell Tolls* that it calls to mind what Ben Jonson said of *The Faerie Queene*: "Spenser writ no language." Hemingway offers a succinct example by translating *"Eras mucho caballo"* as "Thou wert plenty of horse." It is somewhat paradoxical that a writer, having severely cut down his English vocabulary, should augment it by continual importation from other languages, including the Swahili. But this is a facet of the larger paradox that a writer so essentially American should set the bulk of his work against foreign backgrounds. His characters, expatriates for the most part, wander through the ruins of Babel, smattering many tongues and speaking a demotic version of their own. Obscenity presents another linguistic problem, for which Hemingway is not responsible; but his coy ways of circumventing the taboos of censorship are more of a distraction than the conventional blanks. When he does permit himself an expression not usually considered printable, in *Death in the Afternoon,* the context is significant. His interlocutor, the Old Lady, requests a definition and he politely responds: "Madam, we apply the term now to describe unsoundness in abstract conversation or, indeed, any overmetaphysical tendency in speech."

For language, as for literature, his feeling is strongly ambivalent. Perhaps it could be summed up by Pascal's maxim: "True eloquence makes fun of eloquence." Like the notorious General Cambronne, Hemingway feels that one short spontaneous vulgarism is more honest than all those grandiloquent slogans which rhetoricians dream up long after the battle. The disparity between rhetoric and experience, which became so evident during the First World War, prompted the Twenties to repudiate the genteel stylistic tradition and to accept the American vernacular as our norm of literary discourse. "Literary" is a contradiction in terms, for the resultant style is basically oral; and when the semiliterate speaker takes pen in hand, as Hemingway demonstrates in "One Reader Writes"—as H. L. Mencken demonstrated in "A Short View of Gamalielese"—the result is even more artificial than if it had been written by a writer. A page is always flat, and we need perspective to make it convey the illusion of life in the round. Yet the very fact that words mean so much less to us than the things they represent in our lives is a stimulus to our imaginations. In "Fathers and Sons" young Nick Adams reads that Caruso has been arrested for "mashing," and asks his father the meaning of that expression.

> "It is one of the most heinous of crimes," his father answered. Nick's imagination pictured the great tenor doing something strange, bizarre, and heinous with a potato masher to a beautiful lady who looked like the pictures of Anna Held on the inside of cigar boxes. He resolved, with considerable horror, that when he was old enough he would try mashing at least once.

The tone of this passage is not altogether typical of Hemingway. Rather, as the point of view detaches itself affectionately and ironically from the youth, it approximates the early Joyce. This may help to explain why it suggests a more optimistic approach to language than the presumption that, since phrases can be snares and delusions, their scope should be limited to straight denotation. The powers of connotation, the possibilities of oblique suggestion and semantic association, are actually grasped by Hemingway as well as any writer of our time. Thus he can retrospectively endow a cheap and faded term like "mashing" with all the promise and poetry of awakening manhood. When Nick grows up, foreign terms will hold out the same allure to him; like Frederic Henry, he will seek the actuality that resides behind the names of places; and Robert Jordan will first be attracted to Spain as a professional philologist. But none of them will find an equivalence between the word and the thing; and Hemingway, at the end of *Death in the Afternoon,* laments that no book is big enough to do final justice to its living subject. "There was so much to write," the dying writer realizes in "The Snows of Kilimanjaro," and his last thoughts are moving and memorable recollections of some of the many things that will now go unwritten. Walt Whitman stated this challenge and this dilemma, for all good writers, when he spoke of expressing the inexpressible.

II

The inevitable compromise, for Hemingway, is best expressed by his account of Romero's bullfighting style: "the holding of his purity of line through the maximum of exposure." The maximum of exposure —this throws much light upon the restlessness of Hemingway's career, but here we are primarily concerned with the holding of his purity of line. It had to be the simplest and most flexible of lines in order to accommodate itself to his desperate pursuit of material. His purgation of language has aptly been compared, by Robert Penn Warren, to the revival of diction that Wordsworth accomplished with *Lyrical Ballads.* Indeed the question that Coleridge afterward raised might once again be asked: why should the speech of some men be more real than that of others? Today that question restates itself in ideological terms: whether respect for the common man necessitates the adoption of a commonplace standard. Everyone who writes faces the same old problems, and the original writers—like Wordsworth or Hemingway—are those who develop new ways of meeting them. The case of Wordsworth would show us, if that of Hemingway did not, that those who break down conventions tend to substitute conventions of their own. Hemingway's prose is not without precedents; it is interesting to recall that his maiden effort, published by *The Double Dealer* in 1922, parodied the King James Bible. He has his forerunners in American fiction, from Cooper to Jack London, whose conspicuous lack was a style as dynamic as their subject matter. The ring-tailed roarers of the frontier, such as Davy Crockett, were Colonel Cantwell's brothers under the skin; but as contrasted with the latter's tragic conception of himself, they were mock-heroic and serio-comic figures, who recommend themselves to the reader's condescension. Mark Twain has been the most genuine influence, and Hemingway has acknowledged this by declaring—with sweeping generosity—that *Huckleberry Finn* is the source of all modern American literature.

But Mark Twain was conducting a monologue, a virtual *tour de force* of impersonation, and he ordinarily kept a certain distance between his narrative role and his characters. And among Hemingway's elder contemporaries, Ring Lardner was a kind of ventriloquist, who made devastating use of the vernacular to satirize the vulgarity and stupidity of his dummies. It remained for Hemingway—along with Anderson—to identify himself wholly with the lives he wrote about, not so much entering into them as allowing them to take possession of him, and accepting—along with their sensibilities and perceptions—the limitations of their point of view and the limits of their range of expression. We need make no word-count to be sure that his literary vocabulary, with foreign and technical exceptions, consists of relatively few and short words. The corollary, of course, is that every word sees a good deal of hard use. Furthermore, his syntax is informal to the point of fluidity, simplifying as far as possible the already simple system of English inflections. Thus "who" is normally substituted for "whom," presumably to avoid schoolmarmish correctness; and "that," doing duty for "which," seems somehow less prophetic of complexity. Personal pronouns frequently get involved in what is stigmatized, by teachers of freshman composition, as faulty reference; there are sentences in which it is hard to tell the hunter from his quarry or the bullfighter from the bull. "When his father died he was only a kid and his manager buried him perpetually." So begins, rather confusingly, "The Mother of a Queen." Sometimes it seems as if Hemingway were taking pains to be ungrammatical, as do many educated people out of a twisted sense of *noblesse oblige*. Yet when he comes closest to pronouncing a moral, the last words of Harry Morgan—the analphabetic hero of *To Have and Have Not*—seem to be half-consciously fumbling toward some grammatical resolution: "A man . . . ain't got no hasn't got any can't really isn't any way out . . ."

The effectiveness of Hemingway's method depends very largely upon his keen ear for speech. His conversations are vivid, often dramatic, although he comes to depend too heavily upon them and to scant the other obligations of the novelist. Many of his wisecracks are quotable out of context, but as Gertrude Stein warned him: "Remarks are not literature." He can get his story told, and still be as conversational as he pleases, by telling it in the first person. "Brother, that was some storm," says the narrator, and the reader hears the very tone of his voice. In one of Hemingway's critical digressions, he declares that he has always sought "the real thing, the sequence of motion and fact which [*sic*] made the emotion . . ." This seems to imply the clear-cut mechanism of verbal stimulus and psychological response that Eliot formulates in his theory of the objective correlative. In practice, however, Hemingway is no more of a behaviorist than Eliot, and the sharp distinction between motion and emotion is soon blurred. Consider his restricted choice of adjectives, and the heavy load of subjective implication carried by such uncertain monosyllables as "fine" and "nice." From examples on nearly every page, we are struck by one which helps to set the scene for *A Farewell to Arms*: "The town was very nice and our house was very fine." Such descriptions—if we may consider them descriptions—are obviously not designed for pictorial effect. When the Colonel is tempted to call some fishing-boats picturesque, he corrects himself: "The hell with picturesque. They are just dammed beautiful." Where "picturesque" might sound arty and hence artificial, "beautiful"—with "damned" to take off the curse—is permissible because Hemingway has packed it with his own emotional charge. He even uses it in *For Whom the Bell Tolls* to express his aesthetic appreciation of gunfire. Like "fine" and "nice," or "good" and "lovely," it does not describe; it evaluates. It is not a stimulus but a projected response, a projection of the narrator's euphoria in a given situation. Hemingway, in effect, is saying to the reader: *Having wonderful time. Wish you were here.*

In short, he is communicating excitement; and if this communication is received, it establishes a uniquely personal relationship; but when it goes astray, the diction goes flat and vague. Hemingway manages to sustain his reputation for concreteness by an exploring eye for the incidental detail. The one typescript of his that I have seen, his carbon copy of "The Killers" now in the Harvard College Library, would indicate that the arc-light and the tipped-back derby hat were later observations than the rest. Precision at times becomes so arithmetical that, in "The Light of the World," it lines up his characters like a drill-sergeant: "Down at the station there were five whores waiting for the train to come in, and six white men and four Indians." Numbers enlarge the irony that concludes the opening chapter of *A Farewell to Arms* when, after a far from epic invocation, a casual introduction to the landscape, and a dusty record of troops falling back through the autumn, rain brings the cholera which kills "only seven thousand." A trick of multiplication, which Hemingway may have picked up from

Gertrude Stein, is to generalize the specific episode: "They always picked the finest places to have the quarrels." When he offers this general view of a restaurant—"It was full of smoke and drinking and singing"—he is an impressionist if not an abstractionist. Thence to expressionism is an easy step: ". . . the room whirled." It happens that, under pressure from his first American publishers, the author was compelled to modify the phrasing of "Mr. and Mrs. Elliott." In the original version, subsequently restored, the title characters "try to have a baby." In the modified version they "think of having a baby." It could be argued that, in characterizing this rather tepid couple, the later verb is more expressive and no more euphemistic than the earlier one; that "think," at any rate, is not less precise or effectual than "try." But, whereas the sense of effort came naturally, the cerebration was an afterthought.

If we regard the adjective as a luxury, decorative more often than functional, we can well understand why Hemingway doesn't cutivate it. But, assuming that the sentence derives its energy from the verb, we are in for a shock if we expect his verbs to be numerous or varied or emphatic. His usage supports C. K. Ogden's argument that verb-forms are disappearing from English grammar. Without much self-deprivation, Hemingway could get along on the so-called "operators" of Basic English, the sixteen monosyllabic verbs that stem from movements of the body. The substantive verb *to be* is predominant, characteristically introduced by an expletive. Thus the first story of *In Our Time* begins, and the last one ends, with the story-teller's gambit: "there was," "there were." In the first two pages of *A Farewell to Arms* nearly every other sentence is of this type, and the third page employs the awkward construction "there being." There is—I find the habit contagious—a tendency to immobilize verbs by transposing them into gerunds. Instead of writing *they fought* or *we did not feel,* Hemingway writes "there was fighting" and "there was not the feeling of a storm coming." The subject does little more than point impersonally at its predicate: an object, a situation, an emotion. Yet the idiom, like the French *il y a,* is ambiguous; inversion can turn the gesture of pointing into a physical act; and the indefinite adverb can indicate, if not specify, a definite place. Contrast, with the opening of *A Farewell to Arms,* that of "In Another Country": "In the fall the war was always there, but we did not go to it any more." The negative is even more striking, when Frederic Henry has registered the sensations of his wound, and dares to look at it for the first time, and notes: "My knee wasn't there." The adverb is *there* rather than *here,* the verb is *was* rather than *is,* because we—the readers—are separated from the event in space and time. But the narrator has lived through it, like the Ancient Mariner, and now he chooses his words to grip and transfix us. *Lo!* he says. *Look! I was there.*

III

Granted, then, that Hemingway's diction is thin; that, in the technical sense, his syntax is weak; and that he would rather be caught dead than seeking the *mot juste* or the balanced phrase. Granted that his adjectives are not colorful and his verbs not particularly energetic. Granted that he commits as many literary offenses as Mark Twain brought to book with Fenimore Cooper. What is behind his indubitable punch, the unexampled dynamics of Hemingway's style? How does he manage, as he does, to animate this characteristic sentence from "After the Storm"?

> I said "Who killed him?" and he said "I don't know who killed him but he's dead all right," and it was dark and there was water standing in the street and no light and windows broke and boats all up in the town and trees blown down and everything all blown and I got a skiff and went out and found my boat where I had her inside of Mango Key and she was all right only she was full of water.

Here is a good example of Hemingway's "sequence of motion and fact." It starts from dialogue and leads into first-person action; but the central description is a single clause, where the expletive takes the place of the observer and his observations are registered one by one. Hence, for the reader, it lives up to Robert Jordan's intention: "You . . . feel that all that happened to you." Hemingway puts his emphasis on nouns because, among parts of speech, they come closest to things. Stringing them along by means of conjunctions, he approximates the actual flow of experience. For him, as for Marion Tweedy Bloom, the key word is *and,* with its renewable promise of continuity, occasionally varied by *then* and *so.* The rhetorical scheme is *polysyndeton*—a large name for the childishly simple habit of linking sentences together. The subject, when it is not taken for granted, merely puts us in touch with the predicate: the series of objects that Hemingway wants to point out. Even a preposition can turn this trick, as "with" does in this account of El Sordo waiting to see the whites of his enemy's eyes:

> Come on, Comrade Voyager . . . Keep on coming with your eyes forward . . . Look. With a red face and blond hair and blue eyes. With no cap on and his moustache is yellow. With blue eyes. With pale blue eyes. With pale blue eyes with something wrong with them. With pale blue eyes that don't focus. Close enough. Too close. Yes, Comrade Voyager. Take it, Comrade Voyager.

Prose gets as near as it can to physical conflict here. The figure enlarges as it advances, the quickening impression grows clear and sharp and almost unbearable, whereupon it is blackened out by El Sordo's rifle. Each clipped sentence, each prepositional phrase, is like a new frame in a strip of film; indeed the whole passage, like so many others, might have been filmed by the camera and projected on the screen. The course of Harry Morgan's launch speeding through the Gulf Stream, or of Frederic Henry's fantasy ascending the elevator with Catherine Barkley, is given this cinematographic presentation. *Green Hills of Africa* voices the long-range ambition of obtaining a fourth and fifth dimension in prose. Yet if the subordinate clause and the complex sentence are the usual ways for writers to obtain a third dimension, Hemingway keeps his writing on a linear plane. He holds the purity of his line by moving in one direction, ignoring sidetracks and avoiding structural complications. By presenting a succession of images, each of which has its brief moment when it commands the reader's undivided attention, he achieves his special vividness and fluidity. For what he lacks in structure he makes up in sequence, carefully ordering visual impressions as he sets them down and ironically juxtaposing the various items on his lists and inventories. "A Way You'll Never Be" opens with a close-up showing the debris on a battlefield, variously specifying munitions, medicaments, and left-overs from a field kitchen, then closing in on the scattered papers with this striking montage-effect: "group postcards showing the machine-gun unit standing in ranked and ruddy cheefulness as in a football picture for a college annual; now they were humped and swollen in the grass. . . ." It is not surprising that Hemingway's verse, published by *Poetry* in 1923, is recognizably imagistic in character—and perhaps his later heroics are foreshadowed by the subject of one of those poems, Theodore Roosevelt.

In her observant book, *L'Age du roman américain*, Claude-Monde Magny stresses Hemingway's "exaltation of the instant." We can note how this emphasis is reflected in his timing, which—after his placing has bridged the distance from *there* to *here*—strives to close the gap between *then* and *now*. Where Baudelaire's clock said "remember" in many languages, Robert Jordan's memory says: "Now, *ahora, maintenant, heute*." When death interrupts a dream, in "The Snows of Kilimanjaro," the ultimate reality is heralded by a rising insistence upon the word "now." It is not for nothing that Hemingway is the younger contemporary of Proust and Joyce. Though his time is neither *le temps perdu* nor the past nostagically recaptured, he spends it gathering roses while he can, to the ever accelerating rhythm of headlines and telegrams and loudspeakers. The act, no sooner done than said, becomes simultaneous with the word, no sooner said than felt. Hemingway goes so far, in "Fathers and Sons," as to render a sexual embrace by an onomatopoetic sequence of adverbs. But unlike Damon Runyon and Dickens, he seldom narrates in the present tense, except in such sporting events as "Fifty Grand." Rather, his timeliness expresses itself in continuous forms of the verb and in his fondness for all kinds of participial constructions. These, compounded and multiplied, create an ambiance of overwhelming activity, and the epithets shift from El Sordo's harassed feelings to the impact of the reiterated bullets, as Hemingway recounts "the last lung-aching, leg-dead, mouth-dry, bullet-spatting, bullet-cracking, bullet-singing run up the final slope of the hill." More often the meaning takes the opposite turn, and moves from the external plane into the range of a character's senses, proceeding serially from the visual to the tactile, as it does when the "Wine of Wyoming" is sampled: "It was very light and clear and good and still tasted of the grapes."

When Nick Adams goes fishing, the temperature is very tangibly indicated: "It was getting hot, the sun hot on the back of his neck." The remark about the weather is thereby extended in two directions, toward the distant source of the heat and toward its immediate perception. Again in "Big Two-Hearted River," Nick's fatigue is measured by the weight of his pack: ". . . it was heavy. It was much too heavy." As in the movies, the illusion of movement is produced by repeating the same shot with further modification every time. Whenever a new clause takes more than one step ahead, a subsequent clause repeats it in order to catch up. Repetition, as in "Up in Michigan," brings the advancing narrative back to an initial point of reference. "Liz liked Jim very much. She liked it the way he walked over from the shop and often went to the kitchen door to watch him start down the road. She liked it about his moustache. She liked it about how white his teeth were when he smiled." The opaque verb "like," made increasingly transparent, is utilized five more times in this paragraph; and the fumbling preposition "about" may be an acknowledgment of Hemingway's early debt to Gertrude Stein..The situation is located somewhere between a subjective Liz and and objective Jim. The theme of love is always a test of Hemingway's objectivity. When Frederic kisses Catherine, her responses are not less moving because they are presented through his reflexes; but it is her sentimental conversation which leaves him free to ask himself: "What the hell?" At first glance, in a behavioristic formula which elsewhere recurs, Colonel Cantwell seems so hard-boiled that motions are his only emotions: "He saw that his hand was trembling." But his vision is blurred by conventionally romantic tenderness when he contemplates a heroine whose profile "could break your . . . or anyone else's heart." Hemingway's heroines, when they aren't bitches, are fantasies—or rather, the masculine reader is invited to supply his own, as with the weather in Mark Twain's *American Claimant.* They are pin-up girls.

If beauty lies in the eye of the beholder, Hemingway's purpose is to make his readers beholders. This is easily done when the narration is conducted in the first person; we can sit down and drink, with Jake Barnes, and watch Paris walk by. The interpolated chapters of *In Our Time,* most of them reminiscences from the army, employ the collective *we*; but, except for "My Old Man," the stories themselves are told in the third person. Sometimes, to strengthen the sense of identification, they make direct appeal to the second person; the protagonist of "Soldier's Home" is "you" as well as "he"—and, more generally, "a fellow." With the exception of Jake's confessions, that is to say *The Sun Also Rises*, all of Hemingway's novels are written in the *style indirect libre*—indirect discourse which more or less closely follows the consciousness of a central character.[1] An increasing tendency for the author to intrude, commenting in his own person, is one of the weaknesses of *Across the River*. He derives his strength from a power to visualize episodes through the eyes of those most directly involved; for a page, in "The Short, Happy Life of Francis Macomber," the hunt is actually seen from the beast's point of view. Hemingway's use of interior monologue is effective when sensations from the outer world are entering the stream of a character's consciousness, as they do with such a rush at El Sordo's last stand. But introspection is not Hemingway's genre, and the night-thoughts of *To Have and Have Not* are among his least successful episodes. His best are events, which are never far to seek; things are constantly happening in his world; his leg-man, Nick Adams, happens to be the eye-witness of "The Killers." The state of mind that Hemingway communicates to us is the thrill that Nick got from skiing in "Cross Country Snow," which "plucked Nick's mind out and left him only the wonderful, flying, dropping sensation in his body."

IV

If psychological theories could be proved by works of fiction, Hemingway would lend his authority to the long contested formula of William James, which equates emotion with bodily sensation. Most other serious writers, however, would bear witness to deeper ranges of sensibility and more complex processes of motivation than those he sees fit to describe. Some of them have accused Hemingway of aggressive anti-intellectualism: I am thinking particularly of Aldous Huxley. But Huxley's own work is so pure an example of all that Hemingway has recoiled from, so intellectual in the airiest sense, and so unsupported by felt experience, that the argument has played into Hemingway's hands. We have seen enough of the latter to know that he doesn't really hate books—himself having written a dozen, several of which are, and will remain, the best of their kind. As for his refusal to behave like a man of letters, he reminds us of Hotspur, who professes to be a laconic Philistine and turns out—with no little grandiloquence—to be the most poetic character in Shakespeare's play. Furthermore, it is not Hemingway, but the slogan-mongers of our epoch, who have debased the language;

[1] *A Farewell to Arms* is also narrated in the first person.—R.P.W.

he has been attempting to restore some decent degree of correspondence between words and things; and the task of verification is a heavy one, which throws the individual back on his personal resources of awareness. That he has succeeded within limits, and with considerable strain, is less important than that he has succeeded, that a few more aspects of life have been captured for literature. Meanwhile the word continues to dematerialize, and has to be made flesh all over again; the first-hand perception, once it gets written down, becomes the second-hand notation; and the writer, who attains his individuality by repudiating literary affectation, ends by finding that he has struck a new pose and founded another school.

It is understandable why no critique of Hemingway, including this one, can speak for long of the style without speaking of the man. Improving on Buffon, Mark Schorer recently wrote: "[Hemingway's] style is not only his subject, it is his view of life." It could also be called his way of life, his *Lebensstil.* It has led him to live his books, to brave the maximum of exposure, to tour the world in an endless search for wars and their moral equivalents. It has cast him in the special role of our agent, our plenipotentiary, our roving correspondent on whom we depend for news from the fighting fronts of modern consciousness. Here he is, the man who was there. His writing seems so intent upon the actual, so impersonal in its surfaces, that it momentarily prompts us to overlook the personality behind them. That would be a serious mistake; for the point of view, though brilliantly intense, is narrowly focused and obliquely angled. We must ask: who is this guide to whom we have entrusted ourselves on intimate terms in dangerous places? Where are his limitations? What are his values? We may well discover that they differ from our assumptions, when he shows us a photograph of a bullfighter close to a bull, and comments: "If there is no blood on his belly afterwards you ought to get your money back." We may be ungrateful to question such curiosity, when we are indebted to it for many enlargements of our vicarious knowledge; and it may well spring from the callowness of the tourist rather than the morbidity of the *voyeur,* from the American zest of the fan who pays his money to reckon the carnage. When Spain's great poet, García Lorca, celebrated the very same theme, averting his gaze from the spilling of the blood, his refrain was "*Que no quiero verla!*" ("I do not want to see it!").

Yet Hemingway wants to see everything—or possibly he wants to be in a position to tell us that he has seen everything. While the boy Nick, his seeing eye, eagerly watches a Caesarian childbirth in "Indian Camp," the far from impassive husband turns away; and it is later discovered that he has killed himself. "He couldn't stand things"—so runs the diagnosis of Nick's father, the doctor. This, for Nick, is an initiation to suffering and death; but with the sunrise, shortly afterward, youth and well-being reassert themselves; and the end of the story reaffirms the generalization that Hazlitt once drew: "No young man ever thinks he shall die." It is easy enough for such a young man to stand things, for he is not yet painfully involved in them; he is not a sufferer but a wide-eyed onlooker, to whom the word "mashing" holds out mysterious enticements. Hemingway's projection of this attitude has given his best work perennial youthfulness; it has also armed his critics with the accusation that, like his Robert Cohn, he is "a case of arrested development." If this be so, his plight is generalized by the Englishman Wilson, who observes that "Americans stay little boys . . . all their lives." And the object of Wilson's observation, Francis Macomber, would furnish a classic case history for Adler, if not for Freud—the masculine sense of inferiority which seeks to overcome itself by acts of prowess, both sanguinary and sexual. Despite these two sources of excitement, the story is a plaintive modulation of two rather dissonant themes: *None but the brave deserves the fair* and *The female of the species is more deadly than the male.* After Francis Macomber has demonstrated his manhood, the next step is death. The world that remains most alive to Hemingway is that stretch between puberty and maturity which is strictly governed by the ephebic code: a world of mixed apprehension and bravado before the rite of passage, the baptism of fire, the introduction to sex.

Afterward comes the boasting along with such surviving ideals as Hemingway subsumes in the word *cojones*—the English equivalent sounds more skeptical. But for Jake Barnes, all passion spent in the First World War, or for Colonel Cantwell, tired and disgruntled by the Second, the aftermath can only be elegiac. The weather-beaten hero of *Across the River,* which appears in 1950, is fifty years old and uneasily conscious of that fact; whereas "the childish, drunken heroics" of *The Sun Also Rises* took place just about twenty-five years ago. From his spectacular arrival in the Twenties, Hemingway's course has paralleled that of our century; and now, at its midpoint, he balks like the rest of us before the responsibilities of middle age. When, if ever, does the *enfant du siècle,* that *enfant terrible,* grow up? (Not necessarily when he grows a beard and calls himself "Mr. Papa.") Frederic Henry plunges into the Po much as Huck Finn dived into the Mississippi, but emerges to remind us even more pointedly of Fabrice del Dongo in Stendhal's *Chartreuse de Parme,* and of our great contemporary shift from trans-atlantic innocence to old-world experience. Certain intimations of later years are present in Hemingway's earier stories, typically Ad Francis, the slap-happy ex-champ in "The Battler." Even in "Fifty Grand," his most contrived tale, the beat-up prizefighter suffers more than he acts and wins by losing—a situation which has its corollary in the title of Hemingway's third collection, *Winner Take Nothing.* The ultimate article of his credo, which he shares with Malraux and Sartre, is the good fight for the lost cause. And the ultimate protagonist is Jesus in "Today is Friday," whose crucifixion is treated like an athletic feat, and whose capacity for taking punishment rouses a fellow feeling in the Roman soldiers. The stoic or masochistic determination to take it brings us back from Hemingway to his medium, which—although it eschews the passive voice—is essentially a receiving instrument, especially sensitized for recording a series of violent shocks.

The paradox of toughness and sensitivity is resolved, and the qualities and defects of his writing are reconciled, if we merely remember that he was—and still is—a poet. That he is not a novelist by vocation, if it were not revealed by his books, could be inferred from his well-known retort to F. Scott Fitzgerald. For Fitzgerald the rich were different—not quantitatively, because they had more money, but qualitatively, because he had a novelistic interest in manners and morals. Again, when we read André Gide's reports from the Congo, we realize what *Green Hills of Africa* lacks in the way of social or psychological insight. As W. M. Frohock has perceived, Hemingway is less concerned with human relations than with his own relationship to the universe—a concern which might have spontaneously flowered into poetry. His talents come out most fully in the texture of his work, whereas the structure tends to be episodic and uncontrived to the point of formlessness. *For Whom the Bell Tolls*, the only one of his six novels that has been carefully constructed, is in some respects an over-expanded short story. Editors rejected his earliest stories on the grounds that they were nothing but sketches and anecdotes, thereby paying incidental tribute to his sense of reality. Fragments of truth, after all, are the best that a writer can offer; and, as Hemingway has said, "Any part you make will represent the whole if it's made truly." In periods as confusing as the present, when broader and maturer representations are likely to falsify, we are fortunate if we can find authenticity in the lyric cry, the adolescent mood, the tangible feeling, the trigger response. If we think of Hemingway's temperamental kinship with E. E. Cummings, and of Cummings' "Buffalo Bill" or "Olaf glad and big," it is easy to think of Hemingway as a poet. After the attractions and distractions of timeliness have been outdated, together with categorical distinctions between the rich and the poor, perhaps he will be remembered for a poetic vision which renews our interrupted contact with the timeless elements of man's existence: bread, wine, bed, music, and just a few more of the concrete universals. When El Sordo raises his glance from the battlefield, he looks up at the identical patch of the blue sky that Henry Fleming saw in *The Red Badge of Courage* and that looked down on Prince Andrey in *War and Peace*.

Confiteor Hominen :
Ernest Hemingway's Religion of Man

by Joseph Waldmeir

In recent years, critics have become increasingly suspicious that it is necessary to read Ernest Hemingway's work on the symbolic as well as on the story level in order to gain a full appreciation of its art.[1] Since the publication of *The Old Man and the Sea,* the suspicion has become first an awareness, then a certainty. Of all Hemingway's work, this one demands most to be read on both levels; and the story, its details, its method of presentation, are sufficiently similar to the balance of his work as to suggest strongly the possibility of a similar reading and perhaps a similar interpretation.

The Old Man and the Sea is, as story, very good Hemingway. It is swiftly and smoothly told; the conflict is resolved into a struggle between a man and a force which he scarcely comprehends, but which he knows that he must continue to strive against, though knowing too that the struggle must end in defeat. The defeat is only apparent, however, for, as in "The Undefeated," it becomes increasingly clear throughout the story that it is not victory or defeat that matters but the struggle itself. Furthermore, *The Old Man and the Sea,* while reasserting the set of values, the philosophy which permeates all of Hemingway, is built upon the great abstractions—love and truth and honor and loyalty and pride and humility—and again speaks of the proper method of attaining and retaining these virtues, and of the spiritual satisfaction inevitably bestowed upon their holder.

The Christian religious symbols running through the story, which are so closely interwoven with the story in fact as to suggest an allegorical intention on Hemingway's part, are so obvious as to require little more

"Confiteor Hominem: Ernest Hemingway's Religion of Man." From *PMASAL,* XLII (1956), 277-281. Reprinted by permission of The Michigan Academy of Science, Arts, and Letters and of The University of Michigan Press.

[1] The two most recent comprehensive examinations of Hemingway symbolism are: Carlos Baker, *Hemingway: The Writer as Artist* (Princeton: Princeton University Press, 1952), and Philip Young, *Ernest Hemingway* (New York: Rinehart, 1952).

than a listing of them here. The Old Man is a fisherman, and he is also a teacher, one who has taught the boy not only how to fish—that is, how to make a living—but how to behave as well, giving him the pride and humility necessary to a good life. During the trials with the great fish and with the sharks his hands pain him terribly, his back is lashed by the line, he gets an eyepiercing headache, and his chest constricts and he spits blood. He hooks the fish at noon, and at noon of the third day he kills it by driving his harpoon into its heart. As he sees the second and third sharks attacking, the Old Man calls aloud " 'Ay,' " and Hemingway comments: "There is no translation for this word and perhaps it is just such a noise as a man might make, involuntarily, feeling the nail go through his hand and into the wood." [2] On landing, the Old Man shoulders his mast and goes upward from the sea toward his hut; he is forced to rest several times on his journey up the hill, and when he reaches the hut he lies on the bed "with his arms out straight and the palms of his hands up." [3]

The Christian symbolism so evident here shifts from man to fish—a legitimate symbol for Christ since the beginning of Christianity, as it was a legitimate religious symbol before Christianity—and back to man throughout the story. This apparent confusion is consistent not only within the Hemingway philosophy as an example of the sacrificer-sacrificed phenomenon (a point which I will discuss later in this paper) but within formal Christianity as well, if the doctrine of the Trinity be accepted. Furthermore, the phenomenon itself closely parallels the Roman Catholic sacrifice of the Mass, wherein a fusion of the priest-man with Christ takes place at the moment of Transubstantiation.

Along with the Christ symbols, reinforcing them, but depending on them for its importance, is a rather intricate numerology. It is not formalized—neither is the numerology of Christianity—but it is carefully set forth.

Three, seven, and forty are key numbers in the Old and New Testaments, and in the religion, and Hemingway makes a judicious use of them. The Old Man, as the story opens, has fished alone for forty-four famine days and with the boy for forty more. The Old Man's trial with the great fish lasts exactly three days; the fish is landed on the seventh attempt; seven sharks are killed; and, although Christ fell only three times under the Cross, whereas the Old Man has to rest from the weight of the mast seven times, there is a consistency in the equal importance of the numbers themselves.

But, once it has been established that *The Old Man and the Sea* may be read on the symbolic as well as on the story level, a new problem presents itself, a problem which grows out of the nature of the symbolic

[2] Ernest Hemingway, *The Old Man and the Sea* (New York: Scribner, 1952), p. 118.
[3] *Ibid.*, p. 134.

level and out of the disturbing realization that the two levels exist harmoniously in the work. I think that the problem may best be expressed by two questions which the discerning reader must have asked himself as he put *The Old Man and the Sea* down: Is the story, as it appears at first glance to be, a Christian allegory? Has the old master tough guy decided, in the words of Colonel Cantwell, "to run as a Christian"? If neither of these questions can be answered with an unqualified affirmative—and I submit that they cannot—then a further question must be asked: Just what is the book's message?

The answer assumes a third level on which *The Old Man and the Sea* must be read—as a sort of allegorical commentary by the author on all his previous work, by means of which it may be established that the religious overtones of *The Old Man and the Sea* are not peculiar to that book among Hemingway's works, and that Hemingway has finally taken the decisive step in elevating what might be called his philosophy of Manhood to the level of a religion.

Two aspects of the total work, including *The Old Man and the Sea*, must be considered at this point in order to clarify the above conclusion on the one hand, and to answer the questions concerning Hemingway's Christianity on the other.

The first of these aspects is Hemingway's concern with man as man, with man in his relation to things of this world almost exclusively. The other world, God, does not often enter into the thoughts, plans, or emotions of a Hemingway character. God exists—most of the characters are willing to admit His existence, or at least, unwilling to deny it—but not as an immanent Being, not ever benevolent or malevolent.

God is sometimes prayed to by the Hemingway hero at moments of crisis, but His aid or succor are never depended upon, never really expected. Thus we have Jake Barnes in the Cathedral at Pamplona, on the eve of his great trial, praying for everybody he can think of, for good bullfights and good fishing; and as he becomes aware of himself kneeling, head bent, he

> was a little ashamed, and regretted that I was such a rotten Catholic, but realized that there was nothing I could do about it, at least for awhile, and maybe never, but that anyway it was a grand religion, and I only wished I felt religious and maybe I would the next time. . . .[4]

And thus, too, we have the Old Man, who, after twenty-four hours of his monumental struggle have passed, prays for heavenly assistance mechanically, automatically, thinking, "I am not religious," and "Hail Marys are easier to say than Our Fathers." And after forty-five hours, he says:

[4] Hemingway, *The Sun Also Rises* (New York: Scribner, 1926), pp. 99-100.

> "Now that I have him coming so beautifully, God help me to endure. I'll say a hundred Our Fathers and a hundred Hail Marys. But I cannot say them now."
>
> Consider them said, he thought, I'll say them later.[5]

But when the struggle is ended and the full ironic impact of his "victory" is clear, he asks himself what it was that beat him, and answers, "Nothing . . . I went out too far." [6]

He who depends too heavily on prayer, or for that matter on any external aids when faced with a crisis, is not very admirable to Hemingway. In *Death in the Afternoon,* when he wants to describe the unmanliness of a "cowardly bullfighter" girding himself for action, Hemingway places him in church

> in his bullfighting clothes to pray before the fight, sweating under the armpits, praying that the bull will embiste, that is, charge frankly and follow the cloth well; oh blessed Virgin that thou wilt give me a bull that will embiste well, blessed Virgin, give me that bull, blessed Virgin, that I should touch this bull in Madrid to-day on a day without wind; promising something of value or a pilgrimage, praying for luck, frightened sick. . . .[7]

A man must depend upon himself alone in order to assert his manhood, and the assertion of his manhood, in the face of insuperable obstacles, is the complete end and justification of his existence for a Hemingway hero. The Old Man *must* endure his useless struggle with the sharks; Manuel, in "The Undefeated," *must,* in spite of his broken wrist and a terrible goring, go in on the bull six times and accept the horn at last; Jake *must* continue to live as "well" and "truly" and "honestly" as he is able in spite of his overwhelming frustration. And each must face his struggle alone, with no recourse to otherworldly help, for only as solitary individuals can they assert their manhood.

And significantly they must go it alone without regard to otherworldly blame. As far as sin is concerned, Jake would probably say along with the Old Man, "Do not think about sin. It is much too late for that and there are people who are paid to do it. Let them think about it." [8] And Manuel would probably nod agreement.

[5] *The Old Man and the Sea,* p. 96.

[6] *Ibid.,* p. 133.

[7] Hemingway, *Death in the Afternoon* (New York: Scribner, 1932), p. 90.

[8] *The Old Man and the Sea,* p. 116. Hemingway has always had a deep respect for Christians—provided they *live* like Christians. His great abstractions are also great Christian virtues; and when he finds a believer, such as the priest in *A Farewell to Arms* or Anselmo in *For Whom the Bell Tolls,* who lives in accord with the abstractions, he praises him as "a Christian," and adds, for the benefit of the hypocritical, "something very rare in Catholic countries."

There is no evidence of intentional blasphemy in any of his work; the deeply religious are frequently exalted, not in the terms of Christianity, but in Hemingway's own terms. In the one-act play, "Today is Friday," Christ's Manhood is given far

However, in spite of such obvious rejections of otherworldly Christianity in his affirmation of Manhood, Hemingway has formulated as rigid a set of rules for living and for the attainment of Manhood as can be found in any religion. These rules, along with the detailed procedure for their application, constitute the second aspect of Hemingway's total work to be considered in this paper.

The rules are built upon the great abstractions mentioned above. They are so bound up with the procedure for their application that the procedure itself might be considered to be a rule—or better, that neither rules nor procedure exist without one another. Hemingway's philosophy of Manhood is a philosophy of action; a man is honest when he acts honestly, he is humble when he acts humbly, he loves when he is loving or being loved. Thus, taking an awareness of the rules as he has taken an awareness of the abstractions for granted, Hemingway concerns himself primarily with the presentation of procedure. The procedure is carefully outlined; it is meticulously detailed. If no part of it is overlooked or sloughed off, it must result in a satisfying experience almost in and of itself.

This procedure, this ritual—for such is what the procedure actually amounts to—is most clearly evident in Hemingway's treatment of the bullfight. *Death in the Afternoon* is devoted to an evaluation of the manhood of various bullfighters on the basis of their ability to abide by the rules, and to a description of the ritual by means of which they prove possession and communicate the satisfaction to be gained from a proper performance of function to the spectator. War, the prize ring, fishing, hunting, and making love are some of the other celebrations by means of which Hemingway's religio-philosophy of Man is conveyed. But the bullfight is the greatest because, besides possessing, as the others do also, a procedure inviolate, intimately related to the great abstractions, it always ends in death. It assumes the stature of a religious sacrifice by means of which a man can place himself in harmony with the universe, can satisfy the spiritual as well as the physical side of his nature, can atone for the grievous omissions and commissions of his past, can purify and elevate himself in much the same way that he can in any sacrificial religion. The difference between Hemingway's religion of man and formal religion is simply—yet profoundly—that in the former the elevation does not extend beyond the limits of this world, and in the latter, Christianity for example, the ultimate elevation is totally otherworldly.

---

greater importance than His Godhead with no blasphemous overtones. The First Soldier, speaking for Hemingway and offering the highest praise he is capable of, answers, "He was pretty good in there today," each time the cynical Second Soldier minimizes Christ's manliness. The words are not only directly addressed to the cynic, but indirectly to the emotionally disturbed Third Soldier as well, who has had a religious experience which the First cannot share, but which he comprehends and sympathizes with.

The bullfighter is in a sense a priest, performing the sacrifice for the sake of the spectator as well as for his own sake, giving each that "feeling of life and death and mortality and immortality" which Hemingway described in *Death in the Afternoon,* and, as does the Roman Catholic priest on the ideal level, the bullfighter actually places his own life in jeopardy. This curious phenomenon of the sacrificer gambling on becoming the sacrificed serves to clarify the terms of Hemingway's system, rather than, as at first glance it might seem, to confuse them. The bullfighter recognizes the possibility and immanence of death when he steps into the ring, and he must face it bravely. He must perform the sacrifice cleanly, with one true stroke, preserving both his honor and the bull's dignity. If he kills out of malice or out of fear his actions will show it, and the spectator will be distracted from concentration upon the sacrifice to awareness of the man, and no satisfaction will result.

There must be a cognizance of death both from the standpoint of killing and from that of being killed; there must be more than a cognizance actually; there must be an acceptance. Knowledge of death's inevitability so that he does not react to its immediacy, coupled with unconcern for the possibilities of life after death, are necessary attributes of the ideal bullfighter. His aim can extend no further than the great abstractions themselves, how he earns them and how he communicates them. He must realize that it is not *that* one dies but *how* one dies that is important. And equally important, that it is not *that* one kills but *how* one kills.

It is not only in his treatment of the bullfight that this second aspect of Hemingway's total work is evident, though there it may be most immediately apparent. The abstractions, the rules, the ritual, the sacrifice dominate the details of *The Old Man and the Sea* as they dominate those of "The Undefeated" and *The Sun Also Rises.*[9] We are told carefully, painstakingly, how the Old Man performs his function as fisherman; how he prepares for the hoped-for struggle:

[9] With the possible exception of sacrifice, they dominate the details of *Across the River and Into the Trees* as well. If examined in terms of the religion of Manhood, this is not as unsuccessful a book as most critics have claimed. It gives those members of the Order who realize that they will die a natural death a way to meet the problem of dying. Colonel Cantwell still enjoys many of the things that have contributed to the happiness of his life—the beauties of nature and art, the taste of good food and drink, the pleasures of hunting, the give and take of sexual love—and in memory he can experience again the pleasure of fulfilling a soldier's duties.

The reviewers have looked upon this preparation for dying as little more than nostalgic sentimentalism; but even granting that the story tends in this direction, it still fits neatly into the Hemingway religio-philosophical mold. At its climax there is the usual refusal to turn to the supernatural, a more pointed refusal than ever: "You going to run as a Christian?" the Colonel asks himself, and answers, "Maybe I will get Christian toward the end. Yes, he said, maybe you will. Who wants to make a bet on that?" (p. 291)

> Before it was really light he had his baits out and was drifting with the current. One bait was down forty fathoms. The second was at seventy-five and the third and fourth were down in the blue water at one hundred and one hundred and twenty-five fathoms. Each bait hung head down with the shank of the hook inside the bait fish, tied and sewed solid and all the projecting part of the hook, the curve and the point, was covered with fresh sardines. Each sardine was hooked through both eyes so that they made a half-garland on the projecting steel.
>
> . . . Each line, as thick around as a big pencil, was looped onto a green-sapped stick so that any pull or touch on the bait would make the stick dip and each line had two forty-fathom coils which could be made fast to the other spare coils so that, if it were necessary, a fish could take out over three hundred fathoms of line.[10]

We are told how he hooks the fish and secures the line, waiting suspensefully for the fish to turn and swallow the bait, then waiting again until it has eaten it well, then striking, "with all the strength of his arms and the pivoted weight of his body," three times, setting the hook; then placing the line across his back and shoulders so that there will be something to give when the fish lunges, and the line will not break. We are told specifically, in terms reminiscent of such descriptions of the bullfight, how the kill is made:

> The old man dropped the line and put his foot on it and lifted the harpoon as high as he could and drove it down with all his strength, and more strength he had just summoned, into the fish's side just behind the great chest fin that rose high in the air to the altitude of a man's chest. He felt the iron go in and he leaned on it and drove it further and then pushed all his weight after it.[11]

The immanence of death for the sacrificer as well as for the sacrificed, and his total disregard of its possibility, are made clear at the climax of the struggle when the Old Man thinks: "You are killing me, fish . . . Come on and kill me. I do not care who kills who." [12]

It is at this point I think that the questions asked earlier in this paper can be answered. Has Hemingway decided to "run as a Christian"? I think not; the evidence in *The Old Man and the Sea*, with the exeception of the Christian symbolism, indicates that he is no more Christian now than he was when he wrote *The Sun Also Rises*. But the Christian symbolism *is* in the book, and it *does* appear to constitute a Christian religious allegory. Yes, but on a superficial level. The religious allegory, attached to the two aspects of the total body of Hemingway's work as

[10] *The Old Man and the Sea*, pp. 33-34.
[11] *Ibid.*, pp. 103-104.
[12] *Ibid.*, p. 102.

they appear in *The Old Man and the Sea,* which have been the subject of most of my discussion thus far, actually constitute a third level on which *The Old Man and the Sea* must be read—as the allegorical interpretation of the total body of the work.

I said above that Hemingway is no more Christian now than he was thirty years ago; it has been my intention in this paper to show that he was *no less religious* thirty years ago than he is now. The evidence which I have presented adds up to something more than a philosophy or an ethic, the two terms which have most often been used to describe Hemingway's world view; it adds up to what I would call a Religion of Man. Hemingway did not turn religious to write *The Old Man and the Sea.* He has always been religious, though his religion is not of the orthodox, organized variety. He celebrates, he has always celebrated, the Religion of Man; *The Old Man and the Sea* merely celebrates it more forcefully and convincingly than any previous Hemingway work. It is the final step in the celebration. It is the book which, on the one hand, elevates the philosophy to a religion by the use of allegory, and on the other, by being an allegory of the total body of his work, enables us to see that work finally from the point of view of religion.

Hemingway : The Matador and the Crucified

by Melvin Backman

Running through Ernest Hemingway's work, from *In Our Time* to *The Old Man and the Sea,* are two dominant motifs —the matador and the crucified. The matador represents a great force held in check, releasing itself proudly in a controlled yet violent administering of death. The crucified stands for the taking of pain, even unto death, with all of one's courage and endurance so that it becomes a thing of poignancy and nobility. Although it was not until *The Old Man and the Sea* that Hemingway achieved a perfect blending of his two themes, the continual tension and interplay between those forces represented by the matador and the crucified create a pattern in the Hemingway canon against which the individual works of fiction may be profitably studied.

In Our Time sets forth the pain and brutality of our world, recorded apparently without comment in a terse, telegraphic style. Yet underneath the tight-lipped writing a current of protest and repressed brooding threads its secretive way. This is violence caught in the stifled shock of its initial impact. The stories and interchapters have the effect of painful memories of which one must rid himself to exorcise their evil spell, to drive them from the night into the day.

Recoiling from these memories of a sick world, the discharged soldier Nick Adams sought retreat in the Big Two-Hearted River. In this story, Hemingway omits rather ominously all mention of the war and of the people and places of Nick's past, so that a strange aloneness and suspension of time are created. Nick's only function was to fish, to immerse himself so completely in the physical sensations and details of his fishing that there was no need to think. This became, therefore, a strange idyl. Nick called it "the good place," but it was the good place because of its associations with a certain part of his past—fishing and hunting, the river and the woods—which had not been excised from his life as he was trying to do with all the rest. It was as though he wanted to rub out his immediate past and begin clean again here in the woods. But even the woods had been burned over—now there were just charred stumps and black grasshoppers. Yet here amid the shelter and quiet of the trees and the river, with the sun warm on his back and his line trailing in the water, was a moment of separation, of forgetfulness, of peace.

If Nick Adams was trying to withdraw from his world in "Big Two-Hearted River," it was in "Soldier's Home" that the Hemingway protagonist was officially separated. The soldier Krebs found himself hopelessly alienated from the conventional, middle-class American town to which he returned. Living with a kind of flat despair from day to day, holding in abeyance the inevitable decision, he dwelt in uneasy isolation in the midst of his family. Pushed to action finally by family pressure, he decided to sever the last clinging thread of his filial bond. It was a curiously cold, passionless rebellion, as though he had long since worn out his emotions and given up his hope.

In cutting the human bonds that tie one to his world there is the danger of cutting into the very will to live. The threat of this infection hovers over the three stories "Mr. and Mrs. Elliot," "Cat in the Rain," and "Out of Season," each concerned with an American couple characterized by sexual sterility and impotence. Marked by a strangely bloodless discord, without intensity or love, their lives follow a drifting purposeless course. But like green wooded mountains rising abruptly out of barren plains, the descriptions of matadors (interspersed between the stories) emerge in sharp relief:

> When he started to kill it was all in the same rush. The bull looking at him straight in front, hating. He drew out the sword from the folds of the muleta and sighted with the same movement and called to the bull, Toro! Toro! and the bull charged and Villalta charged and just for the moment they became one. Villalta became one with the bull and then it was over. Villalta standing straight and the red hilt of the sword sticking out dully between the bull's shoulders. Villalta, his hand up at the crowd and the bull roaring blood, looking straight at Villalta and his legs caving.

From the unvoiced fears of disintegration of Nick Adams, from the weary despair and apathy of Krebs, and from the scorn, which may mask a secret dread, of the passionless and sterile union of impotent lovers, Hemingway has turned to the violence of the matador.

The theme is developed more fully in *The Sun Also Rises*. If *In Our Time* recorded, for Hemingway, the waves of man's violence effacing the recognizable outline of the shore of one's home, *The*

Sun Also Rises depicts the human wreckage that had been left behind. The time was one of irresponsibility, drunkenness, and promiscuity. As Mike pursued his drunken way, trailing his mounting debts like a banner, Brett preceded her escort, trailing her mounting amours, like a Don Juan turned weary bitch. Jake and Bill Gorton joined in the drunken camaraderie. Yet the endless rounds of drinks seemed to be accompanied by endless rounds of useless quarrels, and the camaraderie was broken by animosities and malice. There was, nevertheless, a certain measure of fellowship, loyalty, and even gaiety. Cohn was outside of it, not merely because he did not belong but because he seemed too self-centered to participate in friendship. Friendship or not, there is no denying the essential futility of their lives. It was a life without purpose or direction, without intensity or passion, without faith in themselves or their world. Nor did they seem truly to believe in the hedonism by which they lived. It seemed that at the bottom of their hearts there lay such a cold dead despair that they drank in order not to think of it; they drank to wind themselves up, like a clock that must be wound every twenty-four hours. So they got through their days.

Whatever fault may be found, however, with the character of these people, it is Cohn for whom Hemingway reserved his most damning portrait. Cohn lacked true identity. His personality was without a core; in place of its center there was only a sickly ego expressing itself in the spurious martyrdom of the weak and self-pitying. Woman-dominated, he was without the vital maleness which Hemingway, like Lawrence, deems absolutely essential to the true man. There was no true pride, no resistance to Cohn. In his love of Brett he was childish in his possessiveness and unmanly in his abject pursuit. What a sharply contrasting picture Hemingway has painted of Pedro Romero as he paid suit to Brett by fighting his bull in front of her.

> Never once did he look up. He made it stronger that way, and did it for himself, too, as well as for her. Because he did not look up to ask if it pleased he did it all for himself inside, and it strengthened him, and yet he did it for her too. But he did not do it for her at any loss to himself.

A polarity has been established between Cohn, unmanly representative of the lost generation, and the primitive, Pedro Romero. When these two fought, the hard male core of the young bullfighter could not be touched by Cohn's punches, and he reduced Cohn to a whimpering child.

Pedro was exempt from the *mal de siècle* that beset the others, for his fighting with the bulls brought him into a fundamental relationship with life, which involved the pitting of his maleness against that of the bull. It is a life and death struggle that reveals not only the steel of his young manhood but a certain passion with which he met life—an intensity, a seriousness, a dedicated quality. Pedro had a place in the scheme of existence—and a role to fulfill. With the instinctive sureness of a primitive who need never question his reason for living, he pursued his natural course. And it was this which even Brett came to recognize. There was an absolute center to him. He did not have to drink, he did not have to keep running away. His inner core was brought into a vital active relationship with life. As Jake commented, it is only a bullfighter who lives life to the hilt, bringing to his work all his courage, intelligence, discipline, and art.

The crisis for Pedro came not in the fight with Cohn but in the invasion of his world by Brett. Jake, the only one of the blighted moderns who was truly aware of this other world, served to bridge them. When he agreed to act as go-between in the proposed seduction of the primitive by this woman of the lost generation, he was knowingly betraying all that the matador represented. No wonder that Montoya, the *aficionado,* no longer acknowledged Jake as one of them, for he knew that the two worlds had to stand forever apart if the bullfight was to retain its truth. Oddly enough, it was Brett's remnant of a conscience that, touched by shamed awareness of the desecration she threatened, brought to an end this unnatural conjunction of two separate worlds.

A purer, more natural kind of love is celebrated in *A Farewell to Arms*. Less sustained in movement and less orchestrated than *The Sun Also Rises, A Farewell to Arms* is a more emotional and subjective novel. It seems to be based upon the memory of a lost love and a lost youth: one's first love, dramatized like that of Romeo and Juliet, destroyed by the "they" that Hemingway in Byronic fashion has cast as the enemy that ever seeks to crush the individual. Although there is no primitive, like Pedro Romero, in this novel, there is, in contrast to the comparatively disillusioned picture of the war, the love itself—tender and idyllic. Glowing with the first flush of the lovers' physical discovery of each other, their love overarches the lovers themselves, who remain essentially passive. Lyrically conceived by the author, it is a small fire of life dampened by a sense of doom and threatened by the cold rain of death.

In *The Sun Also Rises* and *In Our Time,* Pedro Romero and Villalta—as their swords go all the way in, the men leaning after—become one with the bull, united for a single instant by death. This is the "moment of truth." It is an intense, almost an ecstatic, moment of communion, involving an abnegation of self before the final merging. The only other experience analogous to this in Hemingway's work is sexual union. Both are experiences of controlled violence that demand a tight holding on of self until the last moment, then the yielding, merging, and flooding ecstasy. Sexual implications may be seen in the matador's domination of the bull that leads to the climax, the final thrusting of the sword; after the sword's entry the caving in of the bull suggests, by a curious transfer of roles, the collapsed tension, the deathlike state of the spent male after ejaculation. Hemingway usually describes love as the act of becoming one: both Maria and Catherine try to become one with their lovers, Robert Jordan and Frederic Henry. While the killing of the bull ends in union, the making of love, as Hemingway has often remarked, becomes a kind of killing, the good killing. The famous love passage in *For Whom the Bell Tolls,* when the earth seems to move, is so filled with death imagery that it might be taken for a description of dying:

> For him it was a dark passage which led to nowhere, then to nowhere, then again to nowhere, once again to nowhere, always and forever to nowhere, heavy on the elbows in the earth to nowhere, dark, never any end to nowhere, hung on all time always to unknowing nowhere, this time and again for always to nowhere, now beyond all bearing up, up, up and into nowhere, suddenly, scaldingly, holdingly all nowhere gone and time absolutely still and they were both there, time having stopped and he felt the earth move out and away from under them.

The feeling of soaring suggests a mystic ascension and recalls the soaring of the airplane in "The Snows of Kilimanjaro" that symbolized death.

It is this twining of sex and death, both fundamental crises of life, that is central to Hemingway's work. Both killing and sexual union are basic primitive experiences in which the male asserts his will and proves his manhood. In the primitive mind, both love and death are surrounded by religious and fearful influences. Because of a sense of danger and evil attending both marriage and death, ceremonies are instituted and taboos and restrictions imposed as safeguards. And Hemingway—defying Christianity's condemnation of killing and its concept of sex as a sort of necessary sin—has presented love as a mystic ceremonial experience and killing (killing cleanly with honor, pride, and humility) as a spiritual experience.

> Killing cleanly and in a way which gives the esthetic pleasure and pride has always been one of the greatest enjoyments of the human race. . . . When a man is still in rebellion against death he has pleasure in taking to himself one of the Godlike attributes; that of giving it. This is one of the most profound feelings in those men who enjoy killing. These things are done in pride and pride, of course, is a Christian sin, and a pagan virtue.

In a world from which Hemingway has sought to dissociate himself, the only sacred subjects left for him have proved to be love and death—experiences which he has sought to invest with the quality of ancient mysteries.

One remembers the cold rain of *In Our Time* associated with an evil violence, the rain of the fiesta in *The Sun Also Rises* that became part of a Walpurgis-like nightmare, the black rain of the Caporetto retreat and of the death of Catherine Barkley in *A Farewell to Arms*. But in *For Whom the Bell Tolls* there is no rain. The sun dominates the novel—the sun shining through the trees and warming the pine-needled earth. The setting—except for the occasional huddling within the cave, where the atmosphere was close, sullen, as Pablo brooded drunkenly on his lost manhood, as tempers flared darkly, and death stalked ominously—the setting is of the out-of-doors. There love was made and the soldier's death received. And there was the sun, the warm life-giving sun, the sun that heralded the coming of spring after the snow, the sun that was Maria illuminating the life of Robert Jordan. Maria is a child of the sun, with her hair "the color of ripe wheat," her face the "color of burnt gold," and her eyes "gold with the dark flecks in them." And the sun is identified with their love. On the day that Jordan and Maria made love, the hot gold of the sun commingled with the heather smell of the earth and the cropped golden hair of Maria—blending into a Van Gogh-like celebration of the sun so that the pulsing energy of the sun beat through the lovers into the earth and the earth moved. For Robert Jordan, Maria was the sun driving away the night and abolishing loneliness; she was the life that held off death. Finally love itself became a soaring union in which for a moment *la gloria* was realized, a glory like that "in Greco and in San Juan de la Cruz."

That their love should achieve some measure of mystical glory is not completely unprepared for. Maria—her very name suggests the Virgin—was the violated virgin who by the force of her love and will obliterated the violence that had been done her and recaptured her virginity. Borne by the men of Pablo's or rather Pilar's band from the scene of the train disaster, she had been restored to life by Pilar. Although Pilar was her support and protector, all had had a hand in her restoration, and all approached her with tenderness and love. And despite the Loyalists' official disapproval of the Church, it is to the Virgin that many turned in the presence of death.

When El Sordo's band, surrounded and isolated on a hill, were facing annihilation, El Sordo in his last moment thought: "Dying was nothing and he had no picture of it nor fear of it in his mind. But living was a field of grain blowing in the wind." This image of life may suggest association with the recurring description of Jordan's running his hand through Maria's close-cropped hair like the wind blowing through the tawny wheat. But Sordo did not pray; it was Joaquin—the boy who just the day before had been teasing Maria like a brother—who, as the planes swooped down, uttered a "Hail Mary" at the hour of his death. The bombs dropped, splitting the air apart, hitting the earth with a red black roar; "and the earth rolled under him with the roar. Then it came again and the earth lurched under his belly and one side of the hilltop rose into the air and then fell slowly over them where they lay." For him too the earth had moved.

After the action only the enemy was left. Lieutenant Berrendo, riding at the head of the column, thought of his friend Julian, dead on the hill, and prayed to the Virgin for the soul of his friend. At almost the same moment Anselmo caught sight of the enemy column, and frozen by fear he prayed to the "most kind, most sweet, most clement Virgin." Unknowingly these two men, pledged enemies and destined to die the next day, were united in their prayer.

It would seem, then, that while Maria is associated with the sun, and the sun generally with life, she is also associated with the Virgin,[1] and the Virgin with death. Yet in the last chapter—when all that has gone before has led us painstakingly and inevitably to the destruction of the bridge—the sun is curiously twisted together

[1] Other evidence that might be offered is the reference to the "Blessed Virgin of Pilar" in the letter of the cavalryman shot by Robert Jordan. There is also the ambiguous evidence of the Fascists' conferring of the title of "Red Bride of Christ" upon Maria, and the scene in which Maria, in the Mary Magdalen tradition, serves Jordan, "The Lord and Master."

with death. The scene is the opening of the chapter, just prior to the commencement of the Loyalist attack at dawn, the bombing to serve as signal for the blowing of the bridge. Jordan, who had always loved the coming of the sun, lay on the pine-needled earth and watched the first light of the sun dispelling the light mist that obscured the outline of the bridge. As the bridge shone clear in the morning light he heard the bombs drop, and he drew a long breath, as if to expel the lonely feeling that came with the dealing of death, and he prepared to shoot the sentry. The sentry stood in the road with the sun shining on him. "There was no mist on the road now and Robert Jordan saw the man, clearly and sharply, standing there on the road looking up at the sky. The sun shone bright on the trees." And gently Robert Jordan squeezed the trigger. After the death of the sentry came the wiring of the bridge. With the sound of shots in his ear, suspended under the trestle of the bridge, Jordan worked with a tense quick deliberateness against time, lashing the grenades to the girders. But for a moment the noise of the white bubbling stream below him drowned out the war, and looking down he saw a trout nibbling on the chip he had dropped, and through the metal of the bridge he saw the sunlight on the green slope that had been brown but three days ago. It was a green moment of peace that could not be, and it had to yield to the twisting of sun and bridge into destruction.

And the sunlight played over Fernando, the good cigar-store Indian Fernando with all his fine wooden dignity, as he lay wounded against the bank.

> In front of him was one of the whitewashed stones that marked the edge of the road. His head was in the shadow but the sun shone on his plugged and bandaged wound and on his hands that were cupped over it. His legs and his feet also were in the sun. The rifle lay beside him and there were three clips of cartridges shining in the sun beside the rifle.

Then there was Anselmo—loyal Anselmo, the good old man who did not want to kill, believing that killing men was sin—with the wire pulled tight around his fist, waiting for the signal from the *Inglés*. The sun weighed heavy on his back. Then came the blowing of the bridge—and Anselmo lay face down behind the white marking stone, that shone in the sunlight like a common gravestone for the good and the brave.

If the sun represents the exposure that spelled death for some, for Robert Jordan it meant still more. The novel opens with Jordan lying on the pine-needled floor of the forest, planning the destruction of the bridge that arched peacefully over the stream, white in the summer sunlight. And the novel ends:

> Lieutenant Berrendo, watching the trail, came riding up, his thin face serious and grave. His sub-machine gun lay across the saddle in the crook of his left arm. Robert Jordan lay behind the tree, holding onto himself very carefully and delicately to keep his hands steady. He was waiting until the officer reached the sunlit place where the first trees of the pine forest joined the green slope of the meadow. He could feel his heart beating against the pine-needle floor of the forest.

We have come full circle. The pine trees and the sun and Robert Jordan have become inextricably mingled with the giving and receiving of death. Yet there is the moving memory of the love in the hot sunlight and the love on the pine boughs in the cool nights in the sleeping bag. It is as though death in some subtle fashion has not only twisted itself about love but has become a secret forbidden attraction that the Hemingway hero finds hard to resist. But resist it he must, even if resistance requires the inflicting of violence upon others. Or it may be that by his administering of death he takes unconscious revenge for the violence inflicted upon the young manhood of Nick Adams and Jake Barnes and Frederic Henry.

Yet death in this novel is different from death in *The Sun Also Rises* or *Death in the Afternoon.* In those earlier works the dominating point of view was that of the matador, because killing was the means of proving one's manhood. The identification was chiefly with the killer; there was a deep fundamental enjoyment, Hemingway said, to be had from killing. In *For Whom the Bell Tolls,* however, there is an ambiguity of attitude. In only one instance did Robert Jordan identify himself, partially at least, with the desire to kill. This took place at the scene when Robert Jordan and Agustín, tense and still behind their guns, were watching the enemy cavalry depart. Agustín, speaking of the necessity to kill that was on him like "on a mare in heat," said that there was no stronger thing in life. Jordan, in silent thought, called it the Spanish "extra sacrament" that, repressed by Christianity, had welled forth in wars and inquisitions; and Jordan admitted that he too and "all who are soldiers by choice have enjoyed it at some time whether they lie about it or not." Yet throughout the story Jordan never killed with pleasure but always with reluctance. He could not bring himself to "assassinate" Pablo, he shot the sentry with sadness, and his defensive killing of the cavalryman initiated a long searching of his conscience in which he questioned his right to kill. (Even the old man in *The Old Man and the Sea* continues this questioning of one's right to kill.) Jordan's position seems to lie between that of Anselmo and Pablo. Although Agustín had spoken of killing as an instinct, only with Pablo had this "instinct" become an inordinate lust, revealed in the brutally sadistic executions and the blood-drunken slaughter initiated by Pablo during the taking of his town. Part of Robert Jordan—the greater part, it would seem—was in accord with Anselmo, who felt that "in those who like it [killing] there is always a rottenness." Hating to kill, Anselmo is a foil to Pablo in other respects, manifesting loyalty as against treachery, courage as against fear, gentleness as against cruelty. Something of the quality of the old man in "Old Man at the Bridge" invests Anselmo. Idealized, of course, he represents a position toward which part of Hemingway was drawn, just as the priest in *A Farewell to Arms* had served as a similar attraction for Frederic Henry.

But the most crucial experience for Robert Jordan lay not in the killing but in the preparing to be killed. Although he had to face up to his ordeal with courage and dignity, like all the Hemingway heroes who live by the "code," the reason for this code is now made clear. Submerged in the back of Jordan's mind was the guilt of his father's suicide, which compelled Jordan to live in such a manner as to annul his father's cowardice. Just as he had to rid himself of the pistol by which his father had shot himself, so had he to rid himself of his father—that is, to obliterate his father from his consciousness, as if he had never been, and to replace him with his grandfather, the soldier in the family.

Although Jordan must die to make the "code" live, to wipe out the stain of his father's cowardice, may there not be another explanation for his pain and death? Jordan, after all, is but part of a pattern into which all the Hemingway protagonists fall. At the end of *In Our Time* Nick Adams, having been initiated into a painful world, was left in a curious state of suspension; Jake Barnes resigned himself hopelessly to a miserable lot in a futile world; Frederic Henry, stripped by death of his love, was left alone with his despair and misery in a war-torn world. Always the Hemingway protagonist was left alone and always a victim, his world a torturing wheel upon which he was stretched. *Death in the Afternoon, Green Hills of Africa,* and *To Have and Have Not* recorded the seeking of violence as a means of asserting oneself in despite of the world. But Harry Morgan received only pain and death. And death came to

Robert Jordan and Richard Cantwell. This pattern of agony and death, with the protagonist as a sort of crucified victim[2]—is it not a curious complement to the matador going in for the kill? Or are these two faces to a single coin? On one side there is the matador who in his administering of death, Hemingway has said, takes on the attributes of a god. Is there an old primitive truth here: the welding of the act to the unvitiated passion, like an Oedipus rising in pure wrath to strike down his father; the godlike taking to oneself of the power to judge and punish, like a Zeus dealing out divine punishment to a transgressing Prometheus; the mingling of sadism with power, like a Moloch demanding sacrifice? On the other side there is the glorifying of the victim, the seeking of brotherhood out of weakness and life out of death, like a Prometheus transformed into helper of mankind, like a Yahweh become Christ. But Hemingway's works do not reflect any true belief in the glory of martyrdom; they reflect only the tendency to see oneself as victim and life as pain. Nor do they manifest any true desire for brotherhood, for the Hemingway protagonist is always an island, separated by his pain and despair and, in the last resort, by death. In a life that is pain, death may come to represent release—the final sleep that knits up souls, the sleep that cannot be had by a Nick Adams haunted by the nightmare of his wounding, by an old man living with a nameless dread ("A Clean Well-Lighted Place"), or by a Frazer ridden with physical pain. The despair that lies at the bottom of so many of the Hemingway protagonists leads either to passive suffering or to a defiant seeking of violence.

When we reach *The Old Man and the Sea,* we seem to have come a long way from the early works, but there is a pattern into which all of them fall. It is true that the old man is the only hero who is not left alone, at the end of the story, with death or despair. He is old and womanless and humble. Yet in him we have a blending of the two dominant motifs—the matador and the crucified.

At first glance it may not seem that what the matador represents is in the old man too. Yet just as the matador pits himself against the bull, so does Santiago pit himself against the great fish; in their killing they achieve a rebellion against death. In this combat both men must call upon their pride and courage, their skill and knowledge of their craft. Whereas the bullfight terminates with the

[2] Both Robert Jordan and Colonel Cantwell are invested occasionally with a vague Christ symbolism. And in a short early play of Hemingway's, "Today Is Friday," the Roman soldier's comment on the crucified Christ—"He was pretty good in there today"—echoes and reechoes throughout the works.

final sword thrust between the shoulders of the bull, the fight with the fish terminates with the thrusting of the harpoon into his heart. And the old man, his hands lacerated and mushy, raises himself out of his pain to bring down the harpoon, in the same way as the matador Maera in *Death in the Afternoon,* disregarding his broken wrist, goes in for the sixth time over the horns of the bull. Nevertheless, there are differences. The artificial setting of the bullfight, its spectators, and its ceremony leave one with the sense that this is but violence on exhibit, that it is not a natural struggle between man and animal, and that the emotions produced seem strained and self-induced. But Santiago's struggle with the fish is natural. As he says, he was born to be a fisherman and the fish was born to be a fish. The killing of fish is an old accepted livelihood. And the setting for Santiago's struggle is the most natural in the world: overhead move the sun and the stars and the moon; beneath sways the sea, *la mar;* and about the boat move the birds and fish. The sea is the old man's home and the others are his friends and brothers. The old fisherman himself—his skin blotched brown by the friendly sun, his eyes "the color of the sea," the scars on his hands "old as erosions in a fishless desert"—is part of this natural universe. It is a complete and closed universe, a friendly one—its Creator neither hostile nor beneficent but mysteriously just. And the old man talks to the fish and the birds and the stars just as primitive man might have done long ago.

Yet more remarkable than Santiago's killing of the fish is his suffering. (Santiago is Spanish for Saint James—the fisherman, apostle, and martyr from the Sea of Galilee.) Etched on the reader's mind is the image of the old man as he settled against the wood of the bow—the big fish towing, the cord tight across the old man's back—and took his suffering as it came, telling himself, " 'Rest gently now against the wood and think of nothing.' " "The old man rode gently with the small sea and the hurt of the cord across his back came to him easily and smoothly." Suffering and gentle and wood blend magically into an image of Christ on the cross. Then as he was pinned to the bow, dreaming for a few minutes of the lions on the long yellow beach, he woke suddenly with a jerk, the line burning his right hand, his left without feeling. He leaned against the line and tried to brake it, while it burned his back and cut deeply into his left hand. "Just then the fish jumped making a great bursting of the ocean . . . jumped again and again." The straining line pulled the old man face down into the slice of dolphin at the bow. He got his head out of the fish, which was nauseating him, and rose slowly to his knees. Taking the strain with his left hand, he washed the dolphin off his face and let his bleeding right hand trail clean in the salt water, reassuring himself the while, " 'Pain does not matter to a man.' " The fish circled slowly, while "the old man was wet with sweat and tired deep into his bones" and his hands were mushy and he was seeing only in flashes and he was feeling himself go. It was then that he prepared for the kill, pitting "all his pain and what was left of his strength and his long gone pride" against the agony of the fish. When he thrust and pushed his harpoon into the fish's heart, "Then the fish came alive, with his death in him, and rose high out of the water showing all his great length and width and all his power and beauty. Then he fell into the water with a crash that sent spray over the old man and all of the skiff." For a moment after the death of the fish, the tension relaxed, but the pain continued and then the sharks came. " 'Ay,' he said aloud. There is no translation for this word and perhaps it is just a noise such as a man might make, involuntarily, feeling the nail go through his hands and into the wood." He fought the sharks through the afternoon, into the evening and the night, until he was almost dead; but the "pain of life" in his hands and shoulders told him otherwise. He fought until he was weaponless. Then he knew he was beaten and turned the skiff home. The sharks bit into what was left of the great fish, but the old man did not heed them. He was past everything now. Finally sailing into the little harbor, making the boat fast, and stepping ashore, he shouldered the mast and started to climb. "It was then that he knew the depth of his tiredness," as he looked back at the head and the white skeleton of the great fish. He climbed again, bearing his mast like a heavy cross, "and at the top he fell and lay for some time with the mast across his shoulder." He got up again. Then reaching his shack, he put the mast against the wall and lay down on his bed. The next morning the boy found him—"his face down on the newspapers with his arms out straight and the palms of his hands out."

Yet that afternoon the old man was dreaming of the lions on the white beaches of Africa. The dream may represent, as Philip Young has suggested, not only a nostalgic return to the strength of one's youth but also a desire for immortality—like the meaning of the frozen leopard on the summit of Kilimanjaro. Despite the suffering and seeming defeat of the old man, the final effect is that of a triumph which is invested not with the violent ritualized quality of the bullfights of *Death in the Afternoon* or the uneasily insistent and belligerent note of *Green Hills of Africa,* but with a warm autumnal glow. The old man beating off the sharks is like life rebelling against death—as though the old man and the great fish who are lashed together and steering as one toward home, just as earlier they had been bound by the "pain of life," have become the symbol of life; while the sharks (scavengers like the vultures and hyena who are symbols of death in "The Snows of Kilimanjaro") have become the death which must be resisted even though it will win.

Combined with this triumph is a tenderness not usually found in Hemingway's work. For all of Hemingway's glorifying of love between man and woman, too much of the author seemed involved, as Edmund Wilson and Philip Young have noted, with a repudiation of woman. But now in the relation between man and boy, Hemingway achieves a new gentleness. This turning to male companionships seems characteristically American, recalling the paired Huck Finn and Jim, Natty Bumppo and Chingachgook, Ishmael and Queequeg. Curiously, with the exception of Ishmael, they are all variations of primitives. And in Santiago Hemingway has created as fine a primitive as the twentieth century has revealed, one who seems worthy of comparison with Mark Twain's Huck Finn or Jim. But the old man is more richly endowed than most primitives: bearing the name of Saint James, who was fisherman and martyr, he strangely unites the matador and the crucified.

Melvin Backman

The Old Man and the Sea: Hemingway's Tragic Vision of Man

by Clinton S. Burhans, Jr.

I

In *Death in the Afternoon,* Hemingway uses an effective metaphor to describe the kind of prose he is trying to write: he explains that

> if a writer of prose knows enough about what he is writing about he may omit things that he knows and the reader, if the writer is writing truly enough, will have a feeling of those things as strongly as though the writer had stated them. The dignity of movement of an iceberg is due to only one-eighth of it being above water.[1]

Among all the works of Hemingway which illustrate this metaphor, none, I think, does so more consistently or more thoroughly than the saga of Santiago. Indeed, the critical reception of the novel has emphasized this aspect of it: in particular, Philip Young, Leo Gurko, and Carlos Baker have stressed the qualities of *The Old Man and the Sea* as allegory and parable. Each of these critics is especially concerned with two qualities in Santiago—his epic individualism and the love he feels for the creatures who share with him a world of inescapable violence—though in the main each views these qualities from a different point of the literary compass. Young regards the novel as essentially classical in nature; Gurko sees it as reflecting Hemingway's romanticism; and to Baker, the novel is Christian in context, and the old fisherman is suggestive of Christ.[2]

[1] Ernest Hemingway, *Death in the Afternoon* (New York, 1932), p. 183.

[2] On the other hand—though not, to me, convincingly—Otto Friedrich, "Ernest Hemingway: Joy Through Strength," *The American Scholar,* XXVI (Autumn, 1957), pp. 470, 513-30, sees Santiago's experience as little more than the result of the necessities of his profession; Philip Young, *Hemingway* (New York, 1952), p. 100; Leo Gurko, "The Old Man and the Sea," *College English,* XVII, 1, 14 (Oct., 1955); Carlos Baker, *Hemingway* (Princeton, 1956), p. 299.

Such interpretations of *The Old Man and the Sea* are not, of course, contradictory; in fact, they are parallel at many points. All are true, and together they point to both the breadth and depth of the novel's enduring significance and also to its central greatness: like all great works of art it is a mirror wherein every man perceives a personal likeness. Such viewpoints, then, differ only in emphasis and reflect generally similar conclusions—that Santiago represents a noble and tragic individualism revealing what man can do in an indifferent universe which defeats him, and the love he can feel for such a universe and his humility before it.

True as this is, there yet remains, I think, a deeper level of significance, a deeper level upon which the ultimate beauty and the dignity of movement of this brilliant structure fundamentally rest. On this level of significance, Santiago is Harry Morgan alive again and grown old; for what comes to Morgan in a sudden and unexpected revelation as he lies dying is the matrix of the old fisherman's climactic experience. Since 1937, Hemingway has been increasingly concerned with the relationship between individualism and interdependence;[3] and *The Old Man and the Sea* is the culminating expression of this concern in its reflection of Hemingway's mature view of the tragic irony of man's fate: that no abstraction can bring man an awareness and understanding of the solidarity and interdependence without which life is impossible; he must learn it, as it has always been truly learned, through the agony of active and isolated individualism in a universe which dooms such individualism.

II

Throughout *The Old Man and the Sea,* Santiago is given heroic proportions. He is "a strange old man,"[4] still powerful and still

[3] This direction in Hemingway's thought and art has, of course, been pointed out by several critics, particularly by Edgar Johnson in the *Sewanee Review,* XLVIII, 3 (July-Sept., 1940) and by Maxwell Geismar in *Writers in Crisis* (Cambridge, Mass., 1942). With prophetic insight, Johnson says that "the important thing about Hemingway is that he has earned his philosophy, that he has struggled to reach it, overcome the obstacles to attaining it. . . . He has earned the right to reject rejection. For the good, the gentle, and the brave, he now tells us, if they do not try to stand alone and make a separate peace, defeat is not inevitable. His life-blood dripping into the bottom of the boat, Harry Morgan realized it at the end of his career. Philip Rawlings realized it in the blood and terror and tragedy and splendor even of a dying Madrid. Hemingway has realized it there too, and the realization may well be for him the very beginning of a new and more vital career."

[4] Ernest Hemingway, *The Old Man and the Sea* (London, 1952), p. 10.

wise in all the ways of his trade. After he hooks the great marlin, he fights him with epic skill and endurance, showing "what a man can do and what a man endures" (p. 64). And when the sharks come, he is determined " 'to fight them until I die' " (p. 116), because he knows that " 'a man is not made for defeat. . . . A man can be destroyed but not defeated' " (p. 103).

In searching for and in catching his big fish, Santiago gains a deepened insight into himself and into his relationship to the rest of created life—an insight as pervasive and implicit in the old fisherman's experience as it is sudden and explicit in Harry Morgan's. As he sails far out on the sea, Santiago thinks of it "as feminine and as something that gave or withheld great favors, and if she did wild or wicked things it was because she could not help them" (p. 27). For the bird who rests on his line and for other creatures who share with him such a capricious and violent life, the old man feels friendship and love (pp. 26, 46). And when he sees a flight of wild ducks go over, the old man knows "no man was ever alone on the sea" (p. 59).

Santiago comes to feel his deepest love for the creature that he himself hunts and kills, the great fish which he must catch not alone for physical need but even more for his pride and his profession. The great marlin is unlike the other fish which the old man catches; he is a spiritual more than a physical necessity. He is unlike the other fish, too, in that he is a worthy antagonist for the old man, and during his long ordeal, Santiago comes to pity the marlin and then to respect and to love him. In the end he senses that there can be no victory for either in the equal struggle between them, that the conditions which have brought them together have made them one (p. 92). And so, though he kills the great fish, the old man has come to love him as his equal and his brother; sharing a life which is a capricious mixture of incredible beauty and deadly violence and in which all creatures are both hunter and hunted, they are bound together in its most primal relationship.

Beyond the heroic individualism of Santiago's struggle with the great fish and his fight against the sharks, however, and beyond the love and the brotherhood which he comes to feel for the noble creature he must kill, there is a further dimension in the old man's experience which gives to these their ultimate significance. For in killing the great marlin and in losing him to the sharks, the old man learns the sin into which men inevitably fall by going far out beyond her depth, beyond their true place in life. In the first night of his struggle with the great fish, the old man begins to feel a loneliness and a sense almost of guilt for the way in which he has caught him (p. 48); and after he has killed the marlin, he feels no pride of accomplishment, no sense of victory. Rather, he seems to feel almost as though he has betrayed the great fish; "I am only better than him through trickery," he thinks, "and he meant me no harm" (p. 99).

Thus, when the sharks came, it is almost as a thing expected, almost as a punishment which the old man brings upon himself in going far out "beyond all people. Beyond all people in the world" (p. 48) and there hooking and killing the great fish. For the coming of the sharks is not a matter of chance nor a stroke of bad luck; "the shark was not an accident" (p. 99). They are the direct result of the old man's action in killing the fish. He has driven his harpoon deep into the marlin's heart, and the blood of the great fish, welling from his heart, leaves a trail of scent which the first shark follows. He tears huge pieces from the marlin's body, causing more blood to seep into the sea and thus attract other sharks; and in killing the first shark, the old man loses his principal weapon, his harpoon. Thus, in winning his struggle with the marlin and in killing him, the old man sets in motion the sequence of events which take from him the great fish whom he has come to love and with whom he identifies himself completely. And the old man senses an inevitability in the coming of the sharks (p. 101), a feeling of guilt which deepens into remorse and regret. "I am sorry that I killed the fish . . ." (p. 103), he thinks, and he tells himself that "You did not kill the fish only to keep alive and to sell for food. . . . You killed him for pride and because you are a fisherman" (p. 105).

Earlier, before he had killed the marlin, Santiago had been " 'glad we do not have to try to kill the stars' " (p. 74). It is enough, he had felt, to have to kill our fellow creatures. Now, with the inevitable sharks attacking, the old man senses that in going far out he has in effect tried "to kill the sun or the moon or the stars." For him it has not been "enough to live on the sea and kill our true brothers"; in his individualism and his need and his pride, he has gone far out "beyond all people," beyond his true place in a capricious and indifferent world, and has thereby brought not only on himself but also on the great fish the forces of violence and destruction. " 'I shouldn't have gone out so far, fish . . . ,' " he declares. " 'Neither for you nor for me. I'm sorry, fish' " (p. 110). And when the sharks have torn away half of the great marlin, Santiago speaks again to his brother in the sea: " 'Half-fish,' he said. 'Fish that you were. I am sorry that I went too far out. I ruined us both' " (p. 116).

The old man's realization of what he has done is reflected in his apologies to the fish, and this realization and its implications are emphasized symbolically throughout the novel. From beginning to end, the theme of solidarity and interdependence pervades the action and provides the structural framework within which the old man's heroic individualism and his love for his fellow creatures appear and function and which gives them their ultimate significance. Having gone eighty-four days without a catch, Santiago has become dependent upon the young boy, Manolin, and upon his other friends in his village. The boy keeps up his confidence and hope, brings him clothes and such necessities as water and soap, and sees that he has fresh bait for his fishing. Martin, the restaurant owner, sends the old man food, and Perico, the wineshop owner, gives him newspapers so that he can read about baseball. All of this the old man accepts gratefully and without shame, knowing that such help is not demeaning. "He was too simple to wonder when he had attained humility. But he knew he had attained it and he knew it was not disgraceful and it carried no loss of true pride" (pp. 9-10).

Santiago refuses the young boy's offer to leave the boat his parents have made him go in and return to his, but soon after he hooks the great marlin he wishes increasingly and often that the boy were with him. And after the sharks come and he wonders if it had been a sin to kill the great fish, the old man thinks that, after all, "everything kills everything else in some way. Fishing kills me exactly as it keeps me alive." But then he remembers that it is not fishing but the love and care of another human being that keeps him alive now; "the boy keeps me alive, he thought. I must not deceive myself too much" (p. 106).

As the sharks tear from him more and more of the great fish and as the boat gets closer to his home, the old man's sense of his relationship to his friends and to the boy deepens: "I cannot be too far out now, he thought. I hope no one has been too worried. There is only the boy to worry, of course. But I am sure he would have confidence. Many of the older fishermen will worry. Many others too, he thought. I live in a good town" (p. 115). In the end, when he awakens in his shack and talks with the boy, he notices "how pleasant it was to have someone to talk to instead of speaking only to himself and to the sea" (p. 125). This time he accepts without any real opposition the boy's insistence on returning to his boat, and he says no more about going far out alone.

This theme of human solidarity and interdependence is reinforced by several symbols. Baseball, which the old man knows well and loves and which he thinks and talks about constantly, is, of course, a highly developed team sport and one that contrasts importantly in this respect with the relatively far more individualistic bullfighting, hunting, and fishing usually found in Hemingway's stories. Although he tells himself that "now is no time to think of baseball" (p. 37), the game is in Santiago's thoughts throughout his ordeal, and he wonders about each day's results in the *Gran Ligas*.

Even more significant is the old man's hero-worship of Joe DiMaggio, the great Yankee outfielder. DiMaggio, like Santiago, was a champion, a master of his craft, and in baseball terms an old one, playing out the last years of his glorious career severely handicapped by the pain of a bone spur in his heel. The image of DiMaggio is a constant source of inspiration to Santiago; in his strained back and his cut and cramped left hand he, too, is an old champion who must endure the handicap of pain; and he tells himself that he "must have confidence and . . . be worthy of the great DiMaggio who does all things perfectly even with the pain of the bone spur in his heel" (p. 66).

But DiMaggio had qualities at least as vital to the Yankees as his courage and individual brilliance. Even during his own time and since then, many men with expert knowledge of baseball have considered other contemporary outfielders—especially Ted Williams of the Boston Red Sox—to be DiMaggio's equal or superior in terms of individual ability and achievement. But few men have ever earned the affection and the renown which DiMaggio received as a "team player"—one who always displayed his individual greatness as part of his team, one to whom the team was always more important than himself. It used to be said of DiMaggio's value as a "team player" that with him in the line-up, even when he was handicapped by the pain in his heel, the Yankees were two runs ahead when they came out on the field. From Santiago's love of baseball and his evident knowledge of it, it is clear that he would be aware of these qualities in DiMaggio. And when Manolin remarks that there are other men on the New York team, the old man replies: " 'Naturally. But he makes the difference' " (p. 17).

The lions which Santiago dreams about and his description in terms of Christ symbols further suggest solidarity and love and humility as opposed to isolated individualism and pride. So evocative and lovely a symbol is the dream of the lions that it would be foolish if not impossible to attempt its literal definition. Yet it seems significant that the old man dreams not of a single lion, a "king of the beasts," a lion proud and powerful and alone, like the one from which Francis Macomber runs in terror, but of several young lions who come down to a beach in the evening to play together. "He only dreamed of places now and of the lions on the beach. They played like young cats in the dusk and he loved them as he loved the boy" (p. 22). It seems also significant that the old man "no longer dreamed of storms, nor of women, nor of great occurrences, nor of great fish, nor fights, nor contests of strength, nor of his wife" (pp. 21-22)—that is that he no longer dreams of great individualistic deeds like the one which brings violence and destruction on him and on the marlin. Instead, the lions are "the main thing that is left" (p. 65), and they evoke the solidarity and love and peace to which the old man returns after hunting and killing and losing his great fish.

These qualities are further emphasized by the symbolic value of the old fisherman as he carries the mast crosslike up the hill to his shack and as he lies exhausted on his bed. His hands have been terribly wounded in catching the great marlin and in fighting the sharks, and as he lies sleeping "face down on the newspapers with his arms out straight and the palms up" (p. 122), his figure is Christ-like and suggests that if the old man has been crucified by the forces of a capricious and violent universe, the meaning of his experience is the humility and love of Christ and the interdependence which they imply.

Such, then, are the qualities which define man's true place in a world of violence and death indifferent to him, and they are the context which gives the experience of the old fisherman its ultimate significance as the reflection of Hemingway's culminating concept of the human condition—his tragic vision of man. For in his understanding that "it is enough to live on the sea and kill our true brothers," the fellow creatures who share life with us and whom he loves, the old man is expressing Hemingway's conviction that despite the tragic necessity of such a condition, man has a place in the world. And in his realization that in going alone and too far out, "beyond all people in the world," he has ruined both himself and also the great fish, the old man reflects Hemingway's feeling that in his individualism and his pride and his need, man inevitably goes beyond his true place in the world and thereby brings violence and destruction on himself and on others. Yet in going out too far and alone, Santiago has found his greatest strength and courage and dignity and nobility and love, and in this he expresses Hemingway's view of the ultimate tragic irony of man's fate: that only through the isolated individualism and the pride which drive him beyond his true place in life does man develop the qualities and the wisdom which teach him the sin of such individualism and pride and which bring him the deepest understanding of himself and of his place in the world. Thus, in accepting his world for what it is and in learning to live in it, Hemingway has achieved a tragic but ennobling vision of man which is in the tradition of Sophocles, Christ, Melville, and Conrad.

III

It is not enough, then, to point out, as Robert P. Weeks does, that "from the first eight words of *The Old Man and the Sea* . . . we are squarely confronted with a world in which man's isolation is the most insistent truth." [5] True as this is, it is truth which is at the same time paradox, for Santiago is profoundly aware that "no man was ever alone on the sea." Nor is the novel solely what Leo Gurko feels it is—"the culmination of Hemingway's long search for disengagement from the social world and total entry into the natural" (p. 15). If the old man leaves society to go "far out" and "beyond all people in the world," the consciousness of society and of his relationship to it are never for long out of his thoughts; and in the end, of course, he returns to his "good town," where he finds it pleasant "to have someone to talk to instead of speaking only to himself and to the sea." To go no further than Santiago's isolation, therefore, or to treat it, as Weeks does, as a theme in opposition to Hemingway's concern with society, is to miss the deepest level of significance both in his novel and in Hemingway's writing generally.

For, surely, as Edgar Johnson has shown, the true direction of Hemingway's thought and art from the beginning and especially since 1937 has been a return to society—not in terms of any particular social or political doctrine, but in the broad sense of human solidarity and interdependence. If he began by making "a separate peace" and by going, like Santiago, "far out" beyond society, like the old man, too, he has come back, through Harry Morgan's " 'no

[5] Robert P. Weeks, "Hemingway and the Uses of Isolation," *University of Kansas City Review*, XXIV, 125 (Winter, 1957).

man alone,'" Philip Rawlings's and Robert Jordan's "no man is an island," and Santiago's "no man is ever alone on the sea," with a deepened insight into its nature and values and a profound awareness of his relationship to it as an individual.[6]

In the process, strangely enough—or perhaps it is not strange at all—he has come back from Frederic Henry's rejection of all abstract values to a reiteration for our time of mankind's oldest and noblest moral principles. As James B. Colvert points out, Hemingway is a moralist: heir, like his world, to the destruction by science and empiricism of nineteenth-century value assumptions, he rejects equally these assumptions and the principle underlying them—that intellectual moral abstractions possess independent supersensual existence. Turning from the resulting nihilism, he goes to experience in the actual world of hostility, violence, and destruction to find in the world which destroyed the old values a basis for new ones—and it is precisely here, Colvert suggests, in reflecting the central moral problem of his world, that Hemingway is a significant moralist.[7]

But out of this concern with action and conduct in a naturalistic universe, Hemingway has not evolved new moral values; rather, he has reaffirmed man's oldest ones—courage, love, humility, solidarity, and interdependence. It is their basis which is new—a basis not in supernaturalism or abstraction but hard-won through actual experience in a naturalistic universe which is at best indifferent to man and his values. Hemingway tells us, as E. M. Halliday observes, that "we are part of a universe offering no assurance beyond the grave, and we are to make what we can of life by a pragmatic ethic spun bravely out of man himself in full and steady cognizance that the end is darkness." [8]

[6] This development in Hemingway's thought and art is further illustrated in a story which he wrote in 1939 and which, prompted by the recent Cuban revolution, *Cosmopolitan,* CXLVI, 4 (April, 1959), pp. 78-83, has reprinted. "Nobody Ever Dies!" is the story of a Spanish-speaking young man and a girl who have given themselves with selfless devotion to the cause of social liberty in a revolt in Cuba. The young man is trapped and killed by governmental forces, and the girl faces the torture of questioning with "a strange confidence. It was the same confidence another girl her age had felt a little more than five hundred years before in the market place of a town called Rouen."

[7] James B. Colvert, "Ernest Hemingway's Morality in Action," *American Literature,* XXVII (Nov., 1955), pp. 372-85.

[8] E. M. Halliday, "Hemingway's Ambiguity: Symbolism and Irony," *American Literature,* XXVIII (March, 1956), p. 3.

Through perfectly realized symbolism and irony,[9] then, Hemingway has beautifully and movingly spun out of an old fisherman's great trial just such a pragmatic ethic and its basis in an essentially tragic vision of man; and in this reaffirmation of man's most cherished values and their reaffirmation in the terms of our time rests the deepest and the enduring significance of *The Old Man and the Sea*.

Clinton S. Burhans, Jr.

[9] Halliday's comment on Hemingway's ironic method is particularly applicable to *The Old Man and the Sea:* "the ironic gap between expectation and fulfillment, pretense and fact, intention and action, the message sent and the message received, the way things are thought or ought to be and the way things are—this has been Hemingway's great theme from the beginning; and it has called for an ironic method to do it artistic justice" (*ibid.*, p. 15).

Bibliography and Guide to Futher Research

(여기서는 拙著 〈헤밍웨이 文学의 研究〉의
書誌 작성 이후의 書誌만을 든다)

(1) Hanneman, Audre, *Ernest Hemingway: A Comprehensive Bibliography*, Princeton, N.J. : Princeton Univ. Press, 1967.

(2) Arnold, Lloyd, *High on the Wild with Hemingway*, Caldwell, Idaho: The Caxton Printers, Ltd., 1968.

(3) Gurko, Leo, *Ernest Hemingway and the Pursuit of Heroism*, New York: Crowell, 1968.

(4) Hovey, Richard B., *Hemingway: The Inward Terrain*, Seattle: University of Washington Press, 1968.

(5) Joost, Nicholas, *Ernest Hemingway and the Little Magazines: The Paris Years*, Barre, Mass: Barre Publishers, 1968.

(6) Stephens, Robert O., *Hemingway's Nonfiction: The Public Voice*, Chapel Hill: University of North Carolina Press, 1968.

(7) Jobes, Katharine T., ed. *Twenties Century Interpretations of The Old Man and the Sea: A Collection of Critical Essays*, Englewood Cliffs, N.J.: Prentice-Hall, 1968.

(8) Baker, Carlos, *Ernest Hemingway: A Life Story*, New York: Scribner's, 1969.

(9) Benson, Jackson J., *Hemingway: The Writer's Art of Self Defense*, Minneapolis: Univ. of Minnesota Press, 1969.

(10) Peterson, Richard K., *Hemingway: Direct and Oblique*, The Hague: Mouton, 1969.

(11) Seward, William, *My Friend Ernest Hemingway,* New York: A.S. Barnes and Co., 1969.

(12) White, William, *Guide to Ernest Hemingway: An Essay,* Columbus, Ohio: Charles Merrill Publishing Co., 1969.

(13) Wylder, Delbert, *Hemingway's Heroes,* Albuquerque, New Mexico: Univ. of New Mexico Press, 1979.

(14) Young, Philip and Charles Mann, *The Hemingway Manuscripts: An Inventory,* University Park: Pennsylvania State Univ. Press, 1969.

(15) Howell, John, ed. *Hemingway's African Stories: The Stories, Their Sources, Their Critics;* N.Y.: Charles Scribner's,1979.

(16) McCaffery, John K.M., ed. *Ernest Hemingway: The Man and His Work,* New York: Cooper Square Publishers, 1969.

(17) White, William, ed. *The Merrill Studies in The Sun Also Rises,* Columbus, Ohio: Charles Merrill Publishers, 1969.

(18) Gellens, Joy, ed. *Twenties Century Interpretations of A Farewell to Arms: A Collection of Critical Essays,* Englewood Cliffs, N.J.: Prentice-Hall, 1970.

(19) White, William, ed. *The Merrill Checklist of Ernest Hemingway,* Columbus, Ohio: Charles Merrill Publishing Co., 1970.

(20) Farrington, S. Kip, Jr., *Fishing with Hemingway and Glassel,* New York: David MaKay Co., 1971.

(21) Nahal, Chaman, *The Narrative Pattern in Ernest Hemingway's Fiction,* Rutherford, N.J.: Fairleigh Dickinson Univ. Press, 1971.

(22) O'Connor, Richard, *Ernest Hemingway,* New York: McGraw-Hill, American Writers Series, 1971.

(23) Watkins, Floyd, *The Flesh and the Word: Eliot, Hemingway, Faulkner:* Nashville, Tenn: Vanderbilt Univ. Press, 1971.

(24) Watts, Emily S., *Ernest Hemingway and the Arts,* Urbana, Ill.: Univ. of Illinois Press, 1971.

(25) Graham, John, ed. *Merrill Studies in A Farewell to Arms,* Columbus, Ohio: Charles Merrill Publishers, 1971.

(26) Grebstein, Sheldon, *Merrill Studies in For Whom the Bell Tolls,* Columbus, Ohio: Charles Merrill Publishers, 1971.

(27) Baker, Carlos, *Hemingway: The Wrinter as Artist,* Princeton: Princeton Univ. Press, 1972.

(28) Kilmo, Vernon (Jake) and Will Oursler, *Hemingway and Jake: An Extraordinary Friendship,* Garden City, N.Y.: Doubleday, 1972.

(29) McLenden, James, *Papa: Hemingway in Key West,* Miami, Fla.: E.A. Seeman, 1972.

(30) Sutherland, Fraser, *The Style of Innocence: A Study of Hemingway and Callaghan,* Toronto: Clark, Irwin & Co., 1972.

(31) Waldhorn, Arthur, *A Reader's Guide to Ernest Hemingway,* New York: Farrar, Straus, & Giroux, Inc., 1972.

(32) Sarason, Bertram, *Hemingway and the Sun Set,* Washington, D.C.: Micro Card Editions, 1972.

(33) Broer, Lawrence R., *Hemingway's Spanish Tragedy,* University, Alabama: The Univ. of Alabama Press, 1973.

(34) Bruccoli, Matthew and Frazer Clark, Jr., Compilers, *Hemingway at Auction, 1930-1973,* Detroit: Gale Research

Co., 1973.

(35) Grebstein, Sheldon, *Hemingway's Craft,* Carbondale: Southern Illnois Univ. Press, 1973.

(36) Kvarn, Wayne, *Hemingway in Germany: The Fiction, the Legend, and the Critics,* Athens: Ohio Univ. Press, 1973.

(37) Pearsall, Robert B., *The Life and Writings of Ernest Hemingway,* Amsterdam, Holland: Dodopi N.V., 1973.

(38) Shaw, Samuel, *Ernest Hemingway,* New York: Frederick Ungar Publishing Co., 1973.

(39) Waldhorn, Arthur, ed. *Ernest Hemingway: A Collection of Criticism,* New York: McGraw-Hill, 1973.

(40) Castillo-Puche, José Luis, *Hemingway in Spain, Garden* City, New York: Doubleday, 1973.

(41) Benson, Jackson and Richard Astro, eds. *Hemingway In Our Time,* Cornvallis: Oregon State Univ. Press, 1974.

(42) Miller, Madelaine Hemingway, *Ernie,* New York: Crown Publishers, 1974.

(44) Wagner, Linda W., *Ernest Hemingway: Five Decades of Criticism,* East Lansing: Michigan State Univ. Press, 1974.

(45) Blakey, J., *Ernest Hemingway's The Old Man and The Sea,* Toronto, Coles Publishing Company Ltd., 1974.

(46) Hanneman, Audre, *Supplement to Ernest Hemingway: A Comprehensive Bibliography,* Princeton, N.J.: Princeton Univ. Press, 1975.

(47) Wagner, Linda W., *Hemingway and Faulkner: Inventors/ Masters,* Metuchen, N.J.: The Scarecrow Press, 1975.

(48) Benson, Jackson J., ed. *The Short Stories of Ernest He-*

mingway: Critical Essays, Durham, N.C.: Duke Univ. Press, 1975.

(49) Hemingway, Gregory H., *Papa: A Personal Memoir,* Boston: Houghton Mifflin, 1976.

(50) Hemingway, Mary Welsh, *How It Was,* New York: Knopf, 1976.

(51) Donaldson, Scott, *By Force of Will: The Life and Art of Ernest Hemingway,* New York: Viking Press, 1977.

(52) Wagner, Linda W., *Ernest Hemingway: A Reference Guide,* G.K. Hall & Co., Boston, Mass., 1977.

(53) Burgess, Anthony, *Ernest Hemingway and His World,* New York: Charles Scribner's Sons, 1978.

(54) Bruccoli, Matthew J., *Scott and Ernest: The Authority of Failure and the Authority of Success,* Carbondale and Edwardsville, Southern Illinois Univ. Press, 1978.

(55) Nelson, Raymond S., *Hemingway: Expressionist Artist,* The Iowa State Univ. Press, Ames, 1979.

(56) Duggan, MM, & L. Richard, eds. *Fitzgerald/Hemingway Annual,* Gale Research Co., Detroit, Michigan, 1969-1979.

(57) 金炳益 〈헤밍웨이의 思想과 文体〉, 成均館大学校出版部刊, 1978.

(58) 金秉喆 編 〈헤밍웨이〉, 民音社刊, 1979.

김병철

보성전문, 중국국립중앙대학교 대학원 졸업
한국영어영문학회 회장 역임(1979-1981)
중앙대학교 영문과 교수 역임

저서와 역서

「헤밍웨이문학의 연구」, 「헤밍웨이 전기」(1970),
「헤밍웨이 평전」(1974), 「한국근대번역문학사 연구」(1975),
「미국문학사」(1977), 「서양문학번역론」(1978),
「한국근대서양문학사 연구」(1980),
「헤밍웨이 전집」, 「세계문학 전집」 외 다수

E. Hemingway

The Old Man and the Sea

노인과 바다 – 주석과 비평

1판 1쇄 발행 • 1977년 9월 1일
1판 21쇄 발행 • 2025년 3월 5일

편 주 자 • 김 병 철
발 행 인 • 정 현 걸
발 행 • 신 아 사
인 쇄 • 삼일문화
출판등록 • 1956년 1월 5일(제9–52호)
주 소 • 서울특별시 은평구 통일로 59길 4 (2F)
전 화 • (02) 382–6411 팩 스 · (02) 382–6401
홈페이지 • www.shinasa.co.kr
E–mail • shinasa@daum.net

ISBN: 978-89-8396-054-2 (93840)

정가 13,000원